A PILGRIM'S GUIDE
TO THE HOLY LAND

Books by James Martin
Published by The Westminster Press

A Pilgrim's Guide to the Holy Land
Suffering Man, Loving God

A PILGRIM'S GUIDE TO THE HOLY LAND

James Martin

The Westminster Press
Philadelphia

© James Martin 1978

Published by The Westminster Press ®
Philadelphia, Pennsylvania

PRINTED IN THE UNITED STATES OF AMERICA

9 8 7 6 5 4 3 2 1

Library of Congress Cataloging in Publication Data

Martin, James, 1921–
  A pilgrim's guide to the Holy Land.

  British ed. published in 1978 under title: A plain
man in the Holy Land.
  1. Palestine—Description and travel. 2. Christian
pilgrims and pilgrimages—Palestine.
3. Martin, James, 1921–   I. Title.
DS107.4.M3454 1979   915.694′04′5   79-14506
ISBN 0-664-24276-6

915.694
M

Contents

List of Plates

Foreword

The sage once said 'See Naples and die': now the wise man says 'See Jerusalem and Live'. A visit to the Holy Land is the journey of a lifetime.

Happily, air travel has made it possible for thousands of ordinary folk in the midst of busy lives to visit the Land of our Lord. Paradoxically, one can gain more and see more in the company of other pilgrims rather than travelling alone.

Few Scotsmen are better able than my friend Jim Martin to lead Holy Land Pilgrimages, and none is better qualified to describe them. At Glasgow University he was a brilliant Bible scholar. Now with umpteen pilgrimages behind him, he shares his experiences with others.

As an annual leader of parties to Israel, I welcome this book as an aid to future travel and as an introduction for those who journey with me.

I hope readers may be encouraged to take the Journey of a Lifetime. May they *See Jerusalem and Live!*

JAMES CURRIE

Prologue

Not so long ago a visit to the Holy Land was an experience that could fall within the grasp of only a very few people. Recent times have seen a remarkable change. Every year hundreds of quite ordinary people, most of them in quite ordinary financial circumstances, make their way on a tour of the Holy Land.

The mechanics of a Holy Land tour resemble in many ways those of package tours to other countries. But the Holy Land itself is an experience that a visit to no other country can parallel.

This impression is based on my own privileged experience of having led groups to the Holy Land on a number of occasions. It is true that the tours on which I have been engaged have all been pilgrimages and by far the most of my companions have, therefore, been committed Christians. But not all have been so and yet I have observed this fascinating land lay its spell upon everyone of them without exception.

There is something mysterious about the impact made by the Holy Land on its visitors. Perhaps we can best describe it by using a theological term and saying that it has a *numinous* quality. It certainly induces an inevitable and unforgettable response whatever the degree of predisposition present or absent in the traveller.

For Christians, understandably, this is mainly because of the land's association with the life of Jesus. It is not, however, that everything in that land is just as Jesus knew it. Of course there are many changes since those days. Sometimes, indeed, the first-time Christian pilgrim is disappointed and disturbed, even shocked, by the extent to which some particular site may be different from the pious picture he has long been cherishing in his mind.

I well remember, for instance, spending more than a few

minutes one day beneath the cupola of the Church of the Holy Sepulchre with a rather upset minister of the Church of Scotland. He was on his first visit and to his mind the structure that stands today over the place of Jesus's crucifixion was both ugly and unseemly; he was wishing he had never set eyes on it. I tried to point out to him that what mattered most was not the graciousness or gracelessness of anything that was to be seen at any Christian site in the Holy Land today, but what was to be remembered and felt there of Jesus.

This book is meant both for those who have visited the Holy Land and those who hope to visit it; and also for those who never will be there. My hope in writing it is that it may help at least some of them to see more clearly something of the holy thing behind the holy place.

CHAPTER ONE

Flight to Reality

We used to call it Palestine. Frequently we refer to it as the Holy Land. It is, of course, the Land of the Book, the land where Jesus spent his earthly life. That is why it is 'holy'—to Christians anyway—and nowadays part of it is Israel and part of it is occupied Jordan.

I want to try to tell you something about this Holy Land, something, in particular, about the places that Jesus knew and that knew him.

I am going to do this by taking you—in imagination, of course—on a journey to and through this Holy Land. You will not have any expense, except possibly that of buying this book. There will be no need for you to be away from your work; nor any need to abandon any favourite pastime, even for a fortnight. There will be no need even to pack.

Only in imagination. As a result, you will not actually sense the warm sunshine of Tiberias on your back or the soft breeze of Mount Tabor on your face. You will not actually feel the impact of your feet striking that very road above Bethany which Jesus so often walked long ago. You will not actually touch the venerable olive trees in the Garden of Gethsemane or smell the spicy tang of the Souk in the old city of Jerusalem.

But I will try to tell you something about these things and many others; and some of you at least will someday perhaps be able to go to see and experience them for yourselves.

Meantime, let me transport you as best I can in imagination to the Holy Land. I am going to assume—for the purposes of this exercise—that you are going with me on the sort of two weeks' pilgrimage that I have often led and that it is your first visit. I am assuming, too, that you are a 'plain man', like myself.

The very trip out is exciting, not to say thrilling, and not only

3

for those (quite a large proportion of the party) who are flying for the first time. The Alps appear at one and the same time so awesome as their peaks tower majestically above the clouds and so fairy-like as these same peaks are set sparkling in the bright sunlight. The Mediterranean Sea looks serene and beautifully blue from our cruising height of 35,000 feet.

Then there is the sudden coming in upon Tel Aviv from the sea. For some considerable time it has been pitch dark outside the cabin windows, except for the plane's navigation lights on the wing tips. To look down is to see nothing but blackness. Then all at once the blackness is replaced by a fascinating carpet of dancing lights which trace a constantly changing pattern as our aircraft thunders on towards touchdown.

When we disembark at Lod Airport our nostrils are immediately assailed by the heavy sweet scent of orange blossom—unmistakably memorable and ever afterwards to be instantly reminiscent of the Holy Land and all it comes to mean to us.

That first, purely physical, impression, is swiftly followed by another which this time is an affair of mind and heart. As our feet tread the tarmac it suddenly seizes hold of our consciousness that we are actually standing on the very land in which our Lord Jesus spent his earthly life. It is all we can do to keep from kneeling down just where we are in awe and reverence.

As we sit in the bus on its 35-mile journey through the darkness from the airport to Jerusalem, this feeling increases rather than decreases, particularly when the headlights catch for an instant a place name on a signpost, the corner of an orange grove or the outline of a fig tree.

The Holy Land or Palestine (this is simply a more modern form of the original Philistia) is more or less that area covered by modern Israel, including those territories it has occupied since the 1967 war. Lying at the Eastern end of the Mediterranean, it is enclosed by Lebanon, Syria, the River Jordan, Jordan and Egypt.

And it is such a small land really, this Land of the Book, this land to which we have come. Certainly it is small out of all proportion to the importance which has attached to it in world affairs down the centuries and even into our own times, not to speak of its being the cradle of the Christian faith, the very reason for our visit. Now we are actually here.

Our 'home' for our seven days in Jerusalem is to be the Panorama Hotel. Built in 1966, the Panorama stands just off the main road from Jerusalem to Jericho and some four hundred yards from the Garden of Gethsemane.

It stands directly across the valley of the Kedron from Jerusalem and, as its name would suggest, commands a striking outlook. Surprisingly, perhaps, the view is best seen from the dining-room which against all orthodox advice has been sited on the top floor of the building. Its picture windows on three sides reveal a magnificent vista.

In front, across the Kedron, is the Old City, enclosed by its massive stone walls, its appearance dominated by the Dome of the Rock, standing in the middle of the Temple Area and shining brilliantly in the morning or the mid-day sun, its reflection mellowing into a deeper shade of gold in the late afternoon.

On the right the windows show the road dropping from the hotel to the Garden of Gethsemane. We can see also the whole sweep of the Mount of Olives as it rises up past Gethsemane, past the Russian Church, past Dominus Flevit, past Paternoster and so to the Chapel of the Ascension and the very summit of the hill.

Behind, the outlook is towards Bethany and, beyond Bethany, towards the Wilderness, Jericho and the Dead Sea.

I have seen that view at all hours of the day and night: often at sunset, several times at dawn. For anyone to look on that scene at the very beginning of a Holy Land tour is surely to have imprinted on his mind the backcloth for all that is to follow, and at the same time to be gripped by the unique atmosphere surrounding such a trip, if indeed it has not captured him already.

That is why, after breakfast on our first morning, we go up to the hotel's flat roof and view the whole thing on a 360-degree turn.

CHAPTER TWO

Bethlehem: Where it all Began

Bethlehem is our destination on the first morning. Everyone sees this as an obvious, perhaps even inevitable, beginning to our pilgrimage. For this is where it all began, at the first Christmas. Unless, that is, you count the angelic announcement to Mary in Nazareth that she was to bear a very special baby boy. In any event, we shall visit Nazareth later.

And so we set off to Bethlehem which is about six miles from Jerusalem. It is still quite early—around eight o'clock—but the sun has already been up for a long time and by now is quite warm. Already, too, the children are on their way to school.

Bethlehem, as you would expect, is much changed from the 'little town' in which Jesus was born. Nowadays it has some forty thousand inhabitants, nearly all of them Arabs and most of these Roman Catholic Christians.

Bethlehem is a Hebrew name which means 'House of Bread'. Like all of the towns we visit in our pilgrimage, it displays the old and the new cheek by jowl together—in terms of the people and their dress, the houses, the shops, general appearance and character. At one and the same moment you can almost persuade yourself that you have stepped back into the time of Jesus and yet be very much aware of being in the twentieth century.

This is our goal this first morning of ours in the Holy Land—Bethlehem, birthplace of David the King and, of so much greater significance for us, birthplace of Jesus, the King of Kings.

As our bus makes its way out of Jerusalem on the short drive to Bethlehem along a road that was in No Man's Land prior to 1967, we pass a great amount of new building, a visible indication of how the Israelis are consolidating their grip on the territory occupied by them after the Six Days' War. In what seems scarcely any time at all we have reached the outskirts of Bethlehem and we see a shrine very sacred to the Jews at the side of the road. This is the Tomb of Rachel, wife of Jacob.

Just here the road forks. To the right is the way to Hebron. To the left leads us into Bethlehem. We do not, however, enter the centre of the town immediately but first pass beyond it to visit an ancient fortress of Herod a few miles to the south. Herod the Great had a kind of passion for building fortresses in remote places. Masada and Machaerus on the Dead Sea are perhaps the ones that spring first to the minds of most students of the Holy Land. But this one near Bethlehem, usually called the Herodion, is another notable example. The fortified palace that Herod built on the hill-top was itself built on centuries later by the Crusaders who also erected a fortress there.

The bus can take us only about two-thirds of the way up the hill and we have to walk the rest, taking it slowly because of the steepness of the ascent and the gathering heat of the day. But when we reach the top, we find our exertions amply rewarded. Much has been excavated of both the Herodion and the Crusader constructions, and for anyone with a taste for stepping back into the past there is much to sample here.

Even those who reckon that 'ruins' are 'just ruins' wherever you find them have no regrets at climbing to the top. For here we are on the edge of the Wilderness and the view south from this elevation is breathtaking in the chilling grandeur of the frightening desolation that is seen to reach right down to the Dead Sea, glinting far away in the very depths of the earth.

From the Herodion our bus takes us to the Field of Boaz where we all pile out to stand looking across the growing grain towards Bethlehem and reflect on that Old Testament idyll of love and graciousness recorded in the Book of Ruth.

We make still another visit before going into Bethlehem itself. This is to the Fields of the Shepherds, an area very close to the town. It consists of a string of fields lying in the valley which have from earliest times been identified as the region where 'Shepherds watched their flocks by night', that very part of the terrain featured in the gospel stories of the first Christmas.

Adjacent to this area is a village which still bears the name 'The Village of the Watching', and this may be taken as further confirmation that it was in fact the 'night flocking-area' of the district. It was here in the time of Jesus that shepherds gathered their separate flocks into one large flock for the night hours. By doing this they could take turns to rest, or even to sleep, in one of the neighbouring caves while the others kept watch over the sheep. In the morning the flocks were easily disentangled one from another. Each shepherd simply chose himself an elevated vantage point and called his sheep to him. The sheep all knew their own shepherd's voice and responded at once; so that in a very short time the flocks were each heading their various ways to the particular pastures that had been agreed on round the camp-fire the previous evening.

Right in the middle of the Shepherds' Fields is an olive orchard and that is where we go. Not only is it a good place from which to look out across the whole sweep of the Shepherds' Fields but we also see here the remains of the Byzantine Church that once stood at the spot, the cave-shelter which has harboured many shepherds of past centuries and the small but lovely Church of the Angel which has been built on top of that cave.

The orchard with its treasures is bounded by a wall and a gate which is closed when we arrive. When we ring the bell, the custodian comes at once to open up and we find him to be quite the blackest-skinned man any of us is ever likely to see. Inside the orchard we find it exceedingly pleasant with the numerous trees purveying both refreshing shade and attractive fragrance.

Less than a hundred yards' walk from the entrance gate brings us to the excavated remains—not much more than some stumps of columns—of the little Byzantine Church that stood there in the fifth century. From this spot our eyes take in a large part of the two or three mile stretch of plateau which contains the Shepherds' Fields. We observe the vines and the olives and the figs and note how they are arranged in neat terraces. The soil of this country does not yield a living easily so that where fertile soil is to be found the utmost use must be made of it.

Close beside the Byzantine Church excavations is a cave,

referred to usually as 'The Shepherds' Cave'. Some guides will affirm categorically that this was the actual cave used for shelter and for rest during their night vigil by those shepherds to whom first came Christmas tidings of great joy. Our guide—Hamed Essayad from the Mount of Olives—and I are content to say that it would be in such a cave that the Christmas shepherds found refuge and took sleep.

When we pass through the door which is the entrance nowadays we find ourselves in a cave large enough to accommodate some sixty people standing in reasonable comfort. Beneath the roof blackened by long centuries of human use, I read a few verses of Luke's narrative of the shepherds' involvement in the Christmas story and offer a short prayer. Together in the dim light we sing a verse of

> "While humble shepherds watched their flock
> In Bethlehem's plain by night"

before returning to the bright sunlight outside.

Directly above the cave is the tiny Church of the Angel. We crowd in to look at this little shrine whose murals depict the story of the angel's announcement to the shepherds of the Saviour's birth. Outside once more, we catch a glimpse through the trees of Bethlehem high on the hill above us and of the man-made star that towers above the place where Jesus was born. That is where we now head.

The centre of the town is called Manger Square—at one end of which is the Church of the Nativity, built over the traditional birthplace of Jesus. Some people are a little disappointed that there should be a building at all standing on the spot where Jesus was born. But here—as everywhere in the Holy Land— the Christian pilgrim should be prepared to look for the holy thing behind the holy place. It is always there to be found.

The Church of the Nativity was built in A.D. 326 and is probably the oldest Christian church in the world still used for worship. The Emperor Constantine built it at the wish of his mother, Queen Helena, whose researches had convinced her that this was where Jesus had been born. There was a cave here

which Christians had been venerating for at least the previous
two centuries as the birthplace of Jesus. Aware of its sanctity for
Christians, Hadrian had attempted to defile the site by building
a temple to Adonis on top of it. Constantine had this temple
pulled down and put in its place the church which is substantially that which still stands there today.

The large church which the Emperor erected for his mother
and for the Gospel has experienced many alterations in the
centuries since. Enlarged by the Emperor Justinian some two
centuries after Constantine, it remains to this day more or less
as he made it, despite the extensive restorations effected by the
Crusaders in the twelfth century.

The way in is through a low, narrow doorway—so narrow
that only one person at a time may enter, so low that only a
young child does not need to stoop in order to pass through.
There can be few more impressive reminders that anyone who
wishes to pay homage to the Child of Bethlehem must be
prepared to bow his head and humble his heart.

One's first impression inside may be that there is a disap-
pointing bareness in the vast interior. There are not even any
chairs or pews. But a sense of immense and awesome history
soon begins to capture the imagination. First we study the four
rows of red-tinted Corinthian pillars that traverse the church
and divide it into nave and aisles. On some of them we can make
out paintings of saints that were put there by the Crusaders.

Next we turn to the wooden roof high above us. Edward IV
once reconstructed that roof with English oak. He cut down the
oak trees and sent them out to Bethlehem along with tons of
lead. And so the roof of the Church of the Nativity was made
new; that was in 1482. In the seventeenth century, however, the
Turks melted down the lead and used it to make bullets; and
the fact is that the present wooden roof goes back no further
than 1842. I like to think, however, that there may be fragments
in it that used to grow in some English forest back in the late
fourteen-hundreds.

When we bring our eyes back down from the heights of the
roof—a bit reluctantly, perhaps, because the imagination has so

much to conjure with—it is to be shown other treasure beneath
our feet. One of the custodians raises a trapdoor set in the
wooden floor on which we stand and reveals part of the original
flooring of the Constantinian Church. It is about a yard below
our feet and its beautiful mosaic is remarkably well preserved
after all these years.

Fascinating though all this is, it is the actual birthplace of
Jesus that we are particularly anxious to see and so we move to
the far end of the church. There we find the screen, festooned
with ikons, that protectively shuts off the sacrament from the
gaze of ordinary worshippers and is so characteristic of a Greek
Orthodox Church.

For that is what the church is; the Greeks obtaining possession
of it in 1672. The Latins (that is, the Roman Catholics) got a
share in the ownership in 1852 and the southern part belongs to
the Armenians. The Church remains, however, essentially a
Greek Orthodox place of worship which gives rise to an odd
situation. The Greek Orthodox Church celebrates Christmas on
January 6 (for us Western Christians, of course, the last day of
Christmas). This means that, when the majority of the Christian
world is observing the birthday of Jesus on December 25, the
church standing over his birthplace in Bethlehem has still
twelve days to wait before that birthday arrives.

Thoughts of this nature come into our minds as we approach
the screen at the far end of the church but they do not linger.
For almost at once we descend the flight of steps on the right-
hand side which takes us well below the present ground level and
to two caves referred to by some as the 'centre of the world'.

The larger of the two small caves is the Grotto of the Nativity;
the other is the Grotto of the Manger. As the names indicate,
they represent the places where Jesus was born and where the
baby was cradled. No-one can really say with certainty that it
was precisely here that this uniquely important birth took place.
But it must at least have been very near here—the tradition
marking out this spot goes so far back.

In any case, what matters always is the holy thing behind the
holy place. In some places this is easier to discern than in others.

Here the effort required is not very considerable. We gather at one end of the Grotto of the Nativity beside the silver star, set in marble in the floor, which exactly marks the traditional site. Hamed and I say all the factual things we want to say and then we pause for brief devotions.

This is the pattern we follow at most of the Christian sites. But here it is very special.

For a few minutes we have the Grotto of the Nativity all to ourselves—in many of the places in the Holy Land we find ourselves with more company than we would really wish. This makes it all the more impressive and all the more meaningful when we read part of the Christmas story from St. Luke's Gospel, join in a short prayer and then spend some moments meditating in our own fashion, some kneeling beside the star, others just standing quietly by.

Before we ascend the stairs to the church, we sing a verse of 'Away in a Manger' and a verse of 'O, come all ye faithful'. Some of us at least can almost hear the angels singing and almost see the Wise Men's star. One of my party whispers to me as we make our way out, 'Supposing I see nothing else, it has already been well worthwhile to make this trip'.

Once back in the church, we do not retrace our steps to the open air but move through a side door leading directly into the adjoining Roman Catholic Church of St. Catherine.

A flight of steps takes us below St. Catherine's Church into a network of passages and underground chambers. One of these chambers is reckoned to be the very cell where Jerome made his historic translation of the Bible into Latin (the Vulgate). Another is dedicated to the memory of 'The Innocents', the infant children Herod caused to be slaughtered after the first Christmas in his panic to eliminate a suspected candidate for his throne.

We come straight from the Cave of the Innocents back up the steps and outside into the attractive little courtyard attached to St. Catherine's Church. There we take note of a statue of St. Jerome (Hieronymus) with a parchment in his hand—and a skull at his feet, symbol of the transience of human life. With the Grotto of the Nativity and the Cave of the Innocents so

Plate 1. Bethlehem: The Church of the Nativity and the Shepherds' Fields (*pages 7–8*)

Plate 2. The Birthplace of Jesus (*page 12*)

Plate 3.   The Ecce Homo Arch and the Cross above Calvary (*page 15*)

Plate 4. Via Dolorosa. Station V represents the spot where Simon took the Cross (*page* 17)

fresh in our minds, this gives us much to think about.

Thanks to our early start there is still enough of the morning left to permit a quick scamper through part of the old town just across the square from the Church of the Nativity and also a shopping stop. Bethlehem mother-of-pearl and olive wood carvings arouse particular interest.

CHAPTER THREE

The Via Dolorosa and Calvary:
Where it all seemed to end

Having visited the place where Jesus was born, we go next to the place where he died. On the afternoon of the same day we follow the Stations of the Cross to Calvary.

Every Friday afternoon the Roman Catholic clergy lead a procession along the Via Dolorosa in Jerusalem. The Via Dolorosa is the route Jesus is thought to have followed when he was taken from his condemnation before Pontius Pilate to his crucifixion on Golgotha. Street level nowadays is, of course, high above what it was in Jesus's time; and the city has in any case been destroyed and rebuilt several times since then.

All the same, the Via Dolorosa (or Way of Sorrow), tracing its path along the narrow streets of the Old City by way of the Stations of the Cross, may well mark out something like the direction of that last journey of Jesus. Even if it does not, it still is an impressively moving reminder of it and of the great sacrifice of love of which it was part.

On Good Friday the Via Dolorosa procession takes place on a much vaster scale. It starts on this occasion at eleven o'clock in the morning and the numbers participating are swollen to thousands by the addition of a huge concourse of pilgrims from all over the world. Well before eleven o'clock the crowds begin to assemble in the courtyard of an Arab school which is the location of Station One of the Cross. It is from this point that the procession starts and when the time arrives for the procession to move off, the courtyard is jam-packed. The crowd contains a number of pilgrim groups from various countries, many with large wooden crosses which they have brought from their homeland and which they will personally carry along the Via Dolorosa to Calvary.

I once was there on Good Friday. It was a tremendous experience and unforgettable. For us today, however, things are much quieter. It is neither Eastertide nor Friday afternoon; and our progress along the Via Dolorosa is in consequence very much easier.

Before proceeding to the first Station of the Cross we pay a visit to the convent of Ecce Homo, only a few yards away on the other side of the road. This convent belongs to an order called the Sisters of Zion and is built on top of the spot where, beyond much doubt, the Judgement Hall of Pontius Pilate once stood. This explains the name 'Ecce Homo', Latin for 'Behold the man', for these were the words Pilate used of Jesus when he stood on trial before him (John 19: 5).

The Ecce Homo is entered directly from the Via Dolorosa and is marked out very distinctively by a famous arch. Part of an archway erected by the Emperor Hadrian in the second century, the 'Arch of the Ecce Homo' spans the present-day street just beside the convent door and continues inside to the convent church.

Although the Sisters of Zion are a French order, we find ourselves placed in the care of a sister who is Scottish born. She takes us first into the church where we see the continuation of the arch we have already seen outside over the street. Then she escorts us down a flight of steps and shows us the unmistakable remains of a Roman street of long ago.

Her soft Scots accent belies the fact that it is twenty years since she was last in her homeland and delights the ears of the Scots in the group. She explains to us clearly and convincingly her reasons for believing that we are on the very site of Pilate's Palace and standing indeed on an actual part of the courtyard, within yards at most of the spot where Jesus was condemned and from which he started his sad walk to Calvary. When she points out the lines of the soldiers' 'Game of the King' marked out on one of the paving stones, it merely highlights and confirms what we are already persuaded is true—that it was actually here that Pilate said of Jesus, 'Behold the Man'.

Because we have been first to the Ecce Homo, we are better orientated to follow now the Stations of the Cross.

Station One is just across the road from the Ecce Homo. The Antonine Palace, which was Pilate's Jerusalem headquarters, covered an extensive area, including the crypt of the present-day Ecce Homo convent with its famous pavement (Gabbatha or Lithostratos) and reaching over to the present-day Moslem school already mentioned. In the large courtyard of this school a pillar marks the first Station of the Cross and commemorates the condemnation of Jesus.

As we return to the street from Station One, we move a few yards to the right (the Ecce Homo is a yard or two to our left) and find a tablet on the wall indicating Station Two, where Jesus was scourged. Behind the wall at this point is the Chapel of the Flagellation and we take time to pass through its small but lovely garden into the Chapel itself. There the crown of thorns painted on the chancel roof is a vivid statement of what this little shrine commemorates.

Once more out in the bright sunshine and back on the street, we turn right again to pass by the doorway of the Ecce Homo and under its archway. We are now walking along the Via Dolorosa—the nameplate affixed to the wall tells us that this is in fact the name of the street. Like every other street in the Old City of Jerusalem, it is without a pavement at either side and pedestrians often have to press up close against the wall to make room for a motor-car or a laden donkey.

After passing under the arch of the Ecce Homo, the road makes a gentle descent of about a hundred yards and arrives at a T-junction. On the right-hand corner is a municipal hospital which appears to be very busy. The Via Dolorosa turns left and, accordingly, so do we.

Just as we turn the corner we come upon the little chapel which marks Station Three, supposedly where Jesus stumbled for the first time beneath the weight of his cross. A few yards further on is Station Four which indicates where Mary fainted on seeing her son pass by on his way to execution.

As we pick our way along the busy street, past a few shops

and one or two men sitting in the open drawing upon their hubble-bubble pipes, we find that very soon the Via Dolorosa takes another sharp turn, this time to the right. At this corner Station Five marks the spot where Simon of Cyrene was conscripted into carrying our Lord's Cross.

Now the road begins to rise and we ascend by means of a series of steps, widely spaced out, one every two yards or so. Among the shops on either side at this part of the Way of Sorrow are several where we see men working at pieces of olive wood, carving out a cross or a shepherd, perhaps.

Some little distance from Station Five we reach Station Six. A sign on a door indicates this and we notice, too, another sign beside it informing us that this is now a doctor's surgery, giving his name and his consulting hours. Station Six commemorates the kindly action of Veronica who, so the legend goes, took her handkerchief and wiped the face of Jesus as he went on his way to die.

At the top of the ascent we meet another crossing, with the souk (or bazaar) running both right and left. We turn left here but first we take note of the inscription on the wall almost directly opposite which marks Station Seven, where Jesus fell for the second time.

When we turn left into the souk, we are immediately caught up in that wave of humanity which seems to ebb and flow along that street every hour of the waking day. The street is narrow, the crowds are large and progress is slow.

However, we have to proceed only a few steps before we turn aside from the souk to make our way a short distance up the street that feeds into the souk from our right. There, on the wall, a plaque says 'Station VIII'. This Eighth Station of the Cross commemorates Jesus's rebuke to the lamenting women of Jerusalem when he told them to weep not for him but for themselves.

We go no further up that side street but return at once to the souk and resume our forward course, edging and jostling our way through the tightly-packed but mostly extremely good-natured mass of people.

An unexpected interlude comes our way when, just as we are passing, a shopkeeper raises a cry of 'Stop, thief' (at least that is what I take his Arabic to mean) and plunges into the crowd in pursuit of a youth who apparently has been helping himself to some of the shopkeeper's merchandise. In this particular situation the 'chase' which follows is nothing like anything any of us had ever seen before. It rather resembles one fly trying to overtake another in a barrel of treacle. The slow-motion drama does, however, eventually end in the shopkeeper successfully apprehending the thief and marching him back to the shop, despite his voluble protests.

At this point the souk is narrow and not at all brightly il-luminated, because it is roofed over with masonry which, so we are told, was put there by the Crusaders. It is by no means dark but we are somewhat shut off from the dazzling sunshine in which we walked the earlier part of the Via Dolorosa. The dimmer light, combined with the general atmosphere of the souk—the smell of spices, the shops jammed together in such close proximity, the way they are all open to the street with their goods in many instances laid out as if to invite any passing dishonest hand to help itself—engenders an exciting feeling of romanticism in most of the party.

A few, on the other hand, are a little uncomfortable in the press of bodies and are glad when shortly we turn off the souk once more. A flight of stairs on our right-hand side leads us on to the roof of the church that is built over the traditional site of Calvary. Usually referred to as the Church of the Holy Sep-ulchre, this church is otherwise, and more correctly, known as the Church of the Resurrection.

On the roof of the church we come upon the community of the Abyssinians clustered near the dome of the Chapel of St. Helena. These coal-black Christians, who number less than a hundred, live there because it is the closest they are allowed to the Holy Sepulchre. They once—and for a long time—had a place inside the church itself but more than a century ago they were ousted from any share in ownership. Since then they have lived and worshipped here on the roof.

Before we go amongst the Abyssinians—they have a kind of village there of small huts and lean-tos—we take note of Station Nine close by. This marks the falling of Jesus for the third time.

The Abyssinian 'village' is made up of tiny houses that are very humble, even primitive. The Abyssinians themselves, some of whom are to be seen hovering shyly in the background, appear to be friendly and warm-hearted. And so they prove.

Usually pilgrims who come by our route onto the roof of the Holy Sepulchre have to retrace their steps after they have seen the Ninth Station and looked at the Abyssinian settlement. But our guide has other ideas. He speaks to one of the Abyssinian priests—very few of them speak any English whatsoever so that for the rest of us communication is impossible—who readily agrees to admit us to their small chapel in the far corner of this odd 'roof courtyard' area. There the priest reads a part of the Passion narrative in his Ethiopian tongue; I follow by reading the same passage in an English version and offer a short prayer in which I ask God's blessing not only on our steps of pilgrimage but also on our Abyssinian friends.

This done, the priest opens a side door in the chapel which leads us down to the very entrance of the Church of the Holy Sepulchre. Stations Ten, Eleven, Twelve, Thirteen and Four-teen are all inside the building which we are now about to enter.

The Church of the Holy Sepulchre is for many pilgrims, at first sight at least, their biggest disappointment in all the places they visit in the Holy Land.

Calvary, the place where Jesus was crucified to death, is so central to the Gospel story. Few Christians can contemplate actually seeing the very spot without feeling a tug at the heart. When they get there, they find the site of Calvary is covered over by a building which to many seems ugly and to some offensively so.

What they find inside the building usually disappoints them even more. They travel thousands of miles to the place where their Lord was crucified and understandably, even if somewhat unreasonably, they expect to see some kind of 'little green hill' that the centuries have scarcely touched. Instead they find no visible trace of Calvary as it was but everything hidden away beneath the rather unlovely edifice that piety has created.

Nowhere is my constantly re-iterated dictum more relevant than here—'in the holy land you must always try to see the holy thing behind the holy place'. As we enter the church, I urge the group to bear in mind that whether or not they find the structure pleasing, it was here that Jesus gave his life to save the world.

For there is little doubt that this is an authentic site. The first church was erected here at the bidding of the Emperor Constantine. The site was chosen at the direction of Macarius, Bishop of Jerusalem, who believed that it covered the place of crucifixion and also the adjacent place of burial. His contemporaries appear to have been unanimous in their acceptance of his opinion.

The site had been till then occupied by a Temple of Venus which the Emperor Hadrian had built around the year A.D. 136. There is good reason to believe that Hadrian erected his Temple to Venus on this particular spot for the very reason that it was held sacred by the Christians. His purpose was to profane what was a holy place to that hated sect.

It is ironic that what Hadrian may have done with the express purpose of erasing all recollection of the site of Calvary, in fact merely served to fix its location for posterity.

At any rate, at the instigation of Macarius and also by the wish of his mother, Helena, Constantine had the Temple of Venus demolished and the site cleared. This uncovered the rock on which the temple had been built (the Rock of Calvary). An old tomb was also discovered which was believed to be the Tomb of Christ.

Constantine next had a church built to enclose both the Tomb and the Rock which had been cut to form a cube about eighteen feet by fifteen feet. Since its first building the Church of the Holy Sepulchre has shared in the storms that have swept across the Holy City sometimes with very destructive force, suffering damage and even destruction but always eventually being restored.

When the Crusaders captured Jerusalem (in 1099) they

rebuilt the church and the building remains today substantially as they made it, although a great deal of renovation and restoration has been engaged on in recent years and is still proceeding.

In the church itself five different branches of the Christian Church have rights, centuries old, to which they cling jealously. These are the Latins, the Greek Orthodox, the Syrians, the Armenians and the Coptics. The whole thing is somewhat confusing and not a little disturbing sometimes to the first-time visitor.

The church is a vast structure nowadays and we make no attempt to go on an exhaustive tour of its many chapels above and below ground level. Instead we do little more than complete the Stations of the Cross.

Immediately we come through the huge entrance doorway we see a rectangular slab of marble on the floor. This is the Stone of Unction which marks the anointing of the Lord's body for burial. Beside it some rather high and steep steps lead us into twin chapels marking the traditional site of Calvary. The chapel on our right is the Latin or Roman Catholic one. As we stand on its marble floor we are at the Tenth Station which commemorates Jesus being stripped of his clothes. The altar facing us is the location of Station Eleven which marks the nailing of Jesus to the Cross.

The adjoining chapel, on our left, is Greek Orthodox and its altar indicates the traditional site of the Cross, erected on the rock hill of Calvary whose 'cube remnant', as fashioned by Constantine's engineers, is roofed over now by the chapel where we stand. Under the altar table is a round hole in the rock and a Greek Orthodox priest sitting beside it indicates, as he gives us a candle, that this was where the Cross was inserted. Here is the Twelfth Station of the Cross. The Thirteenth is another altar, between the two chapels, which commemorates Mary's receiving the body of her dead son.

For a few minutes the chapels clear of other pilgrims and we have the place more or less to ourselves. As we read a short extract from the crucifixion story and say a brief prayer, we have the opportunity to reflect that whether or not we can ever be sure of the exact spot where it happened, the important thing is to know that Jesus 'died to save us all'.

We descend another flight of steps back to ground level and some forty yards from Calvary we come upon the structure that covers the traditional burial place of Jesus.

This is possibly the least helpful of all the Holy Land shrines. The 'Edicule', to give it its technical name, is an alabaster monstrosity built in the nineteenth century, the successor of a number of earlier shrines on the same site. It houses, first of all, a tiny chamber in which is displayed to view what purports to be a small piece of the actual stone that was used to seal the tomb of Jesus. Beyond this is another small chamber which contains, running along the whole length of the right hand side, a cracked marble slab which covers a stone shelf that is claimed to be the very shelf on which the body of Christ was laid and all that remains now of the original rock of his tomb. This is the Fourteenth Station of the Cross.

As we go into the Holy Sepulchre four at a time (for no more can conveniently be accommodated), we cannot help wishing that it had been left by Constantine and succeeding generations as nearly as possible in its original state, uncovered and unadorned. At the same time, despite the—to us—unhelpful trappings with which centuries of devotion have surrounded this place, we are deeply moved to think that we stand at the very spot where the events of the first Easter took place. Across the centuries we hear again the words of the young man in the tomb, 'He is risen'; and our hearts respond exultantly, 'He is risen indeed'.

As we leave the Church of the Holy Sepulchre, some are puzzled by the fact that this site of Calvary should be within the walls of the Old City when the Bible makes it so clear that Jesus was crucified outside the city. The explanation is simple; and Constantine, Macarius and the rest, after all, were well aware of what the Bible said. The walls of the city do not today follow exactly the lines they did in the time of Jesus. They have, as a matter of fact, changed course several times since then in the course of the various vicissitudes that have befallen Jerusalem. The traditional site of Calvary and of the Tomb, as marked by the Church of the Holy Sepulchre, was outside the walls of Jerusalem as they were in our Lord's time. There is little doubt that, when we stand in the Chapel of Calvary and visit the Holy Sepulchre, we are at the very place where Jesus died and rose again.

Some, nevertheless, have felt impelled from time to time to look for alternative sites outside the present city walls. Several have been canvassed but today only one has any support. This is the Garden Tomb and the adjacent cliff face, known as Gordon's Calvary because of its association with General Gordon of Khartoum fame.

Before returning to our hotel, we visit this 'other Calvary'. It lies not far from the Damascus Gate, the main entrance to the old city. The Garden Tomb is a most pleasing site—it is, in fact, a large and lovely garden, beautifully tended—and very many pilgrims find it one of the most devotionally helpful places they visit in their tour of the Holy Land.

We gather first on a raised stone platform at one end of the Garden Tomb, overlooking the bus station, which is throbbing with activity and exceedingly noisy with the constant sounding of horns. Behind the bus station rises a little cliff. This is the place that General Gordon and others have suggested as the site of Calvary.

The suggestion is given a certain measure of romantic support by the fact that the face of the cliff, viewed from certain angles, may convey the clear impression of a skull. I say 'romantic' support because, even if we were to assume that the contours of the hill face had not substantially altered in nineteen centuries, nowhere in the Gospel narratives is it suggested that Golgotha ('the place of a skull') was so called because of its appearance.

From here we walk leisurely through the garden paths to the Tomb. This is an early burial place of the rolling stone type and cut out of the rock face, as was that tomb of Joseph's in which Jesus was laid. We know that the true location of the happenings of the first Easter is almost certainly where the Church of the

Holy Sepulchre now stands. We know also that the tomb before us probably does not go quite as far back as the time of Jesus anyway. Nevertheless it is still a profoundly moving experience to step inside and see the chamber where the dead were laid.

This operation has also to be conducted a few at a time because of the limitations of space. When all have been in and out again, we read part of the Easter story and say a prayer of thanksgiving that, wherever exactly the Easter events occurred, the fact is that Jesus lives. In the splendidly fitting environment of the Garden Tomb the Easter message never seemed more real. For, as Colin Morris once said in a television programme, 'what the Garden Tomb lacks in archaeological support, it more than makes up for in atmosphere'.

Plate 5. Gordon's Calvary and the Garden Tomb (*page* 23)

Plate 6.   The Garden Tomb (*page 23*)

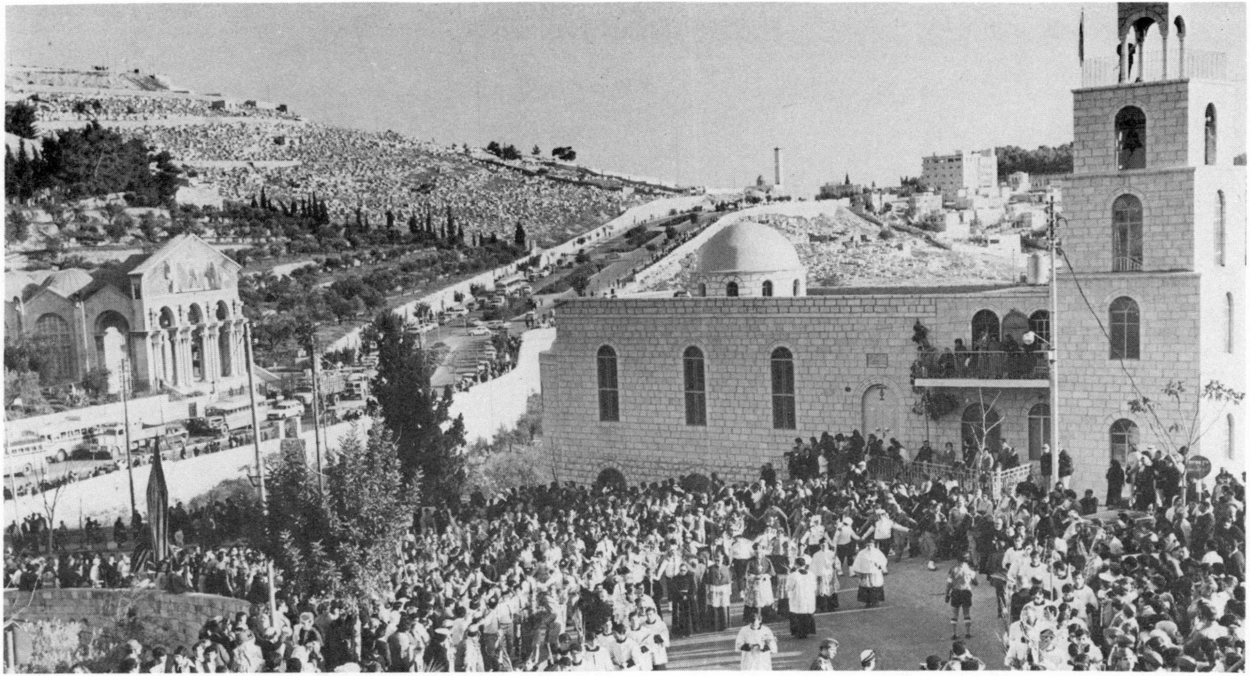

Plate 7. Palm Sunday procession in Jerusalem (*page 27*)

Courtesy Israel Government Tourist Office

Plate 8. The Mount of Olives (*page 27*)

CHAPTER FOUR

The Palm Sunday Walk:
In the very footsteps of Jesus

To the Christian pilgrim the Holy Land speaks of Jesus and of
the Bible nearly all the time. Some places speak of him more
vividly and more pointedly than others. At times the pilgrim is
aware that he is standing where the Lord once actually stood or
walks where his feet once actually trod.

Such is our experience when we walk by the hill road from
Bethany over the top of the Mount of Olives and down the other
side to Gethsemane and the Kedron Valley.

For this surely is the very same path that Jesus often used in
the days of his earthly life. The track winding its way up the
hillside from Bethany is without doubt the self-same route that
men ascending that hill have used from the beginning of human
time.

It is, then, beyond question one part of today's Holy Land
that knew the tread of Jesus's feet when he was on earth. To
walk up that path is truly to walk where Jesus walked. That is
why it is such a thrill the next day to follow that way from
Bethany which Jesus walked many times: but certainly and
notably on the first Palm Sunday.

Bethany lies some three miles from Jerusalem on the road to
Jericho and we make our way by bus to the heart of the village.
Here we find, immediately adjacent to the road, the Church of
St. Lazarus, built in 1953 on the traditional site of the house of
Martha and Mary and Lazarus. This handsome building is
interesting not only for itself and its attractive murals telling
the story of the resurrection of Lazarus but also for the relics
attached to it. There are mosaics dating back to the Byzantine
Church which once occupied the site. There is an inscription

that testifies to the presence in the area of the Tenth Roman Legion, 'Fretensis', which Titus left in occupation of the ruins of Jerusalem and its environs after the destruction of the city by his army in A.D. 70. There is an ancient olive press consisting in part of a cedar trunk two thousand years old.

From the church a fairly steep path ascends the slope. About fifty yards above the church an opening in the hillside is marked as the Tomb from which Jesus brought out Lazarus alive. Those whose energy and agility are a match for their curiosity follow me into the gloom and down a steep flight of stairs. Well below present-day ground level we come to the old burial place over which was built the church erected here in Byzantine times.

When we climb back up the steps and emerge once more into the dazzling sunshine, we find the rest of the group gathered round Hamed, our guide, as he demonstrates how to use a 'David's sling' which he has taken from the pile that a vendor is offering for sale. Inserting a round stone in the pouch of the sling and sliding thumb and forefinger into the loops at either end, Hamed whirls the sling round his head in increasingly rapid circles. Suddenly he releases one end and the stone soars high into the air almost faster and further than our eyes can follow, before plummeting safely to earth almost at the very spot that Hamed had previously indicated.

In response to our gasps of admiration, Hamed says, 'I'm not very good with the sling. One of those shepherds, he is able to kill a bird in flight'. We understand a little better how the shepherd boy David overcame the giant Goliath.

Pushing on, we follow the ancient track as it meanders steadily upwards and halt every now and then to look back on Bethany as it drops below us. As we walk, we see here and there a lizard sunning itself on a stone; we see some tares—bearded darnel—among the wheat; we see 'lilies of the field' in abundance; we see, despite the rough and unpromising nature of the terrain, a lot of olive and fig and almond trees.

About halfway up the hillside we come—where 'two ways meet'—to Bethphage and the little church that commemorates Jesus's mounting the donkey. This is the starting point of the great procession that takes place every year on Palm Sunday. As well as visiting the church, we visit the orchard that grows behind it, for it contains an interesting first-century tomb of the rolling-stone type.

From here on the way up the hill is a modern road with a tarmacadam surface and we are really quite glad of this because the ascent is now noticeably steeper. As we continue upwards a breathtaking view unfolds behind us of the Wilderness, with the Dead Sea glinting beyond and the mountains of Moab standing sentinel at its back.

When we reach the top of the hill and climb the steps of the mosque there to stand on its roof, we discover that the panorama before us is even more thrilling. We are now on the very crest of the Mount of Olives and there in front of us is the Holy City. The Dome of the Rock glitters in the sunshine and Gethsemane snuggles into the corner of our vision on the near side of the Kedron Valley.

In the courtyard below us is the small circular building which has been erected on the traditional site of the Ascension. The Mohammedans, strange as it seems, accept the story of the Ascension of Christ while rejecting the story of his Resurrection; and they are the custodians of this shrine. Inside we encounter one of the most bizarre 'relics' anyone could ever fear to see. A depression in the rock, admittedly not unlike the shape of a human foot, is claimed by some to be the footprint of Christ.

We do not linger long over this and now begin the descent of the Mount of Olives. Soon we come to the Church of the Paternoster. Built to commemorate the teaching by Jesus to his disciples of his model prayer, it carries that 'Lord's Prayer', inscribed on tiles round the cloisters, in no less than 53 different languages.

Continuing our descent of Olivet, we note the mass of Jewish graves on the face of the hill below the American Inter-Continental Hotel. These have all been made here since the Six Days' War of 1967 but they are not all of people who have died during that period. Every year sees a number of Israelis bring the remains of loved ones from their original place of interment to be reburied here on the slopes of the Mount of Olives facing across to the Holy City.

A few yards further down the slope is the Church of Dominus Flevit, one of the most pleasing of all the shrines it is our pleasure to visit. Beautifully sited and beautifully fashioned, Dominus Flevit ('The Lord wept') commemorates, as its Latin name would imply, our Lord's weeping over Jerusalem because of its refusal to listen to his loving appeal. 'How often would I have gathered your children together as a hen gathers her brood under her wings, and you would not'. (Luke 13: 34). The altar in the tiny sanctuary is fronted by a mosaic which depicts a hen gathering her chickens under her wings and the dome of the chapel is in the shape of a tear-drop.

The terrace outside the church affords a magnificent outlook over the Temple Area and the rest of the Old City. In the foreground is the Kedron Valley and to our right and slightly below us are the onion-shaped domes of the Russian Orthodox Church of Gethsemane. Below that again is the Garden of Gethsemane to which we now head.

At the very foot of the Mount of Olives and separated from the main highway only by a high wall, the Garden of Gethsemane is in the care of the Franciscans, custodians—and invariably splendid in their custodianship—of so many of the Christian shrines in the Holy Land. In the time of Jesus the name Gethsemane ('oil press') was applied to an area covering a considerable part of the lower reaches of the Mount of Olives. The Garden of Gethsemane today is only a small section of that area but, in confining its reverence to this, Christian tradition almost certainly acted correctly. When Jesus brought his disciples out of the city and across the Kedron on the night of his betrayal he was most unlikely to have gone any more than a short distance up the opposite slope before drawing aside for his Agony.

In the Garden of Gethsemane, accompanied by a number of carefully tended flowers and shrubs, are twenty-four olive trees. Sixteen of these were planted by the holy fathers only a few years ago. The other eight are very old. Some have thought—H. V. Morton shared the belief—that they may go right back to the time of Jesus. It is extremely unlikely that any of them does but there is this interesting thing to note. It is said that a healthy olive tree lives for about eight hundred years and that it does not die until it has produced a virile young shoot to take its place. This makes the eight old olive trees standing in the Garden of Gethsemane today the grandchildren of the very trees that witnessed Jesus agonising on the night before his Cross.

Beside the Garden is the Franciscans' Church of All Nations. Its title, if we want to be precise, is really the Church of the Agony but everyone knows it as the Church of All Nations because it was built by contributions from all over the world. The interior is rather dark—the windows are not of glass but of coloured alabaster—but deeply impressive.

In front of the altar is that spur of the native rock which is known as the Rock of the Agony and which, tradition says, is where Jesus knelt in his agony of prayer the night that Judas betrayed him with a kiss. On the wall behind the altar mosaics represent the story of the drama played out in Gethsemane that night. In the various little domes in the roof high above other mosaics designate the various nations that contributed to the erection of the church. On the floor at various points we are able to lift protecting covers and see pieces of the original mosaic floor of the Byzantine church that was built on the same site in the fifth century.

Back outside, we linger for a moment in the Garden, looking up through the olive trees to the bulk of the Old City of Jerusalem towering above us. In imagination we see Jesus praying beneath the trees, being arrested, being hustled out of the Garden, across the Kedron, up the opposite slope; and we follow him to Caiaphas, to Pilate, to Calvary. But for the time being this is only in imagination and we make our way slowly and thoughtfully up the Jericho Road to our hotel, less than half a mile away.

CHAPTER FIVE

Jericho, Qumran and the Dead Sea

Our next journey is to Jericho and we discover that when the Bible speaks of going '*down* to Jericho' it means what it says. Jerusalem stands 1,300 feet above sea-level, Jericho 2,300 feet below, and there is only about twenty miles between them. In that short distance, therefore, the descent is some 3,600 feet.

Again it is around eight o'clock in the morning when we pile into our bus. As far as Bethany the road is familiar because we travelled this way only yesterday. From Bethany onwards we are in fresh territory.

The road to Jericho is nowadays pretty straight and wide. But, even without the remains of the old road, sometimes on one side, sometimes on the other, showing us how much more winding and how much more narrow the route used to be, it would still be very easy to visualise the vulnerability of travellers in ancient days, particularly if journeying alone.

Not only in ancient days. The Jerusalem to Jericho road had a reputation as a brigands' paradise that continued well into this century. In his book *In the Steps of the Master* (published first in 1934) H. V. Morton describes how he was planning a trip from Jerusalem to Jericho and was warned to return before dark for fear of falling foul of a certain notorious brigand named Abu Jildah who was active on that road at that time. And Morton was making the trip by motor-car!

There is no doubt that this reputation was highly deserved. When Jerome in the fifth century called it 'The Bloody Way', he named it very aptly. We can readily imagine robbers lying in wait at one of the many defiles or round one of the many sharp turnings that used to characterise the road.

As a result, the famous Parable of the Good Samaritan is already vividly in our minds even before we come to the traditional site of the inn that features in the story. Nowadays it is no more than a deserted building beside a heap of ruins, tenanted only by the man who sells postcards and soft drinks to passing trade like ourselves. But it is very likely that there was an inn of sorts on this very spot in the time of Jesus; and that it was in the Lord's mind when he told his parable.

The site is roughly halfway between Jerusalem and Jericho. It stands a little off the road, on the right-hand side as we make the descent to Jericho, and we make a short stop to inspect it. A sign above the door is marked 'The Inn of the Good Samaritan'. We pass through the entrance and a kind of hallway behind—this is where the soft drinks and the postcards are on sale. On the other side of this porch another door admits us to a vast courtyard, bare except for one or two mounds of rubble and a dried-up well in the centre.

We gather against the high wall on the far side, utilising what little shade there is, and read the passage of Scripture which is in all our minds. Despite the desolation of our immediate surroundings—made to seem all the more desolate to me because I cannot help thinking of my first visit here, before the 1967 War, when this was a Police post and the courtyard housed some superbly beautiful Arab steeds—somehow the story of the Good Samaritan becomes more vividly real than ever before.

Back in the bus, we resume our journey to Jericho. As we drop further towards sea level, the terrain gets wilder and more bleak and the heat of the day intensifies. We see no human habitations now except for some distinctively black Bedouin tents here and there, sometimes singly, more often in groups. By now the wilderness looks really formidable and rather frightening; and as we get nearer to the Dead Sea the increasing salt content in the ground makes the sand look whiter and whiter. Before we reach the Dead Sea we come to a fork in the road and follow the signpost to Jericho. There are in fact two Jerichos, close together, Old and New, ancient and modern. It is modern Jericho we come to first and it certainly makes us sit up and take notice. Its lush greenness is in such contrast to the fearsome desolation of the wilderness in which it is set.

It is the River Jordan that makes the difference, of course, for we are very close to it here. But what a difference! Jericho is as fertile as the surrounding landscape is barren. As we drive through the main street we cannot help being profoundly impressed by the abundance of fruit trees and other growing things; while the splendour of the bougainvillaea, the jacarandra and the flame trees makes a special impact. At the corner of the street is a fruit vendor who is an old friend of Hamed's—and of mine. When we come to his shop, with the fruit displayed in bright abundance on trestles on the pavement, we stop the bus and disembark for a drink of fresh orange juice. On such a day this seems a first-class idea even from within our air-conditioned bus. When we step out on to a street that is 820 feet below sea level to be greeted by a wall of air that feels as though it has come straight from a furnace, the orange juice idea acquires a heightened attraction. Our drinks, each made before our eyes by the pressing of no fewer than four oranges, are perhaps the most delectable ever drunk. None of us, at any rate, is prepared to make a case for the likelihood of nectar having any finer taste.

This, however, is only an interlude, no matter how pleasant; we are really more concerned to visit Old Jericho. It is only about two miles further and in no time we are there. The tel (or mound) of ancient Jericho rises quite steeply from the roadside where the bus deposits us; and we climb up leisurely in the heat to inspect the excavations.

A number of archaeological investigations have been carried out on this site, the most famous, as well as the most recent, being that of Kathleen Kenyon some twenty years ago. These have established ancient Jericho as far and away the oldest city in the world, going back about ten thousand years. We look down with considerable awe at the tower revealed by the excavations, itself some ten thousand years old and the oldest building in the world.

Some distance behind the excavations to the north rises a high, steep cliff. This is the Mount of Temptation, traditionally the place where Jesus underwent his ordeal of testing by the devil. With difficulty, for it blends so well into the cliff face, we pick out the Greek monastery of the Temptation halfway up the precipice, appearing to adhere to the sheer mountainside by nothing short of magic.

On our right, that is to the west, is a totally different scene. It is an abandoned refugee camp. Hundreds upon hundreds of primitive homes stretch into the distance. Up till the 1967 war this camp teemed with life, the home of many thousands of displaced Palestinians. Now not one of its dwellings is occupied, the former inhabitants having all fled across the Jordan.

We are not far from that stretch of the River Jordan where, according to tradition, Jesus was baptised by John. Before June 1967 we could have gone to that spot, but the river is now the effective border between Israel and Jordan and is out of bounds to all tourism.

Consequently we head straight for Qumran. Returning through modern Jericho, we rejoin the road south and soon find ourselves on the Dead Sea. A journey of just a few miles along the shore brings us to the Qumran excavations and the location of those caves in which the Dead Sea Scrolls were found in 1947. These Scrolls are various Hebrew writings, particularly some ancient copies of a few Old Testament books in whole or in part; and they were discovered in a most romantic fashion.

It began with a Bedouin goatherd rejoicing in the exotic name of Muhammed the Wolf. He was herding his goats among the cliffs at the northern end of the Dead Sea. One of the goats strayed away and he was forced to climb up the cliffside to retrieve it. For some reason he flung a stone into a cave above his head—some say it was in the prosecution of his search for the wandering goat, others that it was no more than the idle tossing of a stone into an inviting opening. The significant thing is that he did it.

How startled he was when his stone-pitching ploy was immediately followed by the unmistakable sound of something breaking in the depths of the cave. Anyone who recalls a childhood incident featuring a ball and a broken window will know fairly accurately how that shepherd lad felt, and will not be surprised at his reaction! He ran away.

It was not long before his courage returned—and he came back to investigate, bringing another lad for company. In the cave they found several tall jars, strange-looking to them but of an appearance very familiar now throughout the world. Inside the jars they found rolls of manuscript wrapped in linen and coated with pitch.

It was the spring of 1947 and this was how the first of the Dead Sea Scrolls emerged again into the light of day after being in hiding for nineteen centuries. The rest of the story is even more outlandish and extremely fascinating but this is not the place to tell it. It is enough to say that after this first discovery others followed.

When the nature and value of these first scrolls were appreciated, the multitude of caves honeycombing that area were subjected to intensive search. Hundreds of fragments of manuscript of varying sizes were found, as well as many other items of archaeological interest. Eleven caves in particular were found to have been the repositories for manuscripts and these have been numbered—prosaically but adequately—one to eleven, in order of their investigation.

It became quickly apparent that the various manuscripts must have been part of a library which had been dispersed among the caves for safe-keeping, probably in face of attack and expected defeat. And so it was considered a good idea to 'do a dig' at an old ruin nearby, almost on the shore of the Sea. Whatever was here was almost completely buried, the only thing sticking up above ground level being part of a stone wall; but it was decided to excavate in the hope of finding at least some clue to the place of origin of the scrolls.

No-one could have foreseen that this endeavour would be so richly rewarded. What was uncovered was the remarkably well-preserved remains of a monastery of Essenes (a somewhat ascetic sect of the first century A.D.). What we now call 'The Dead Sea Scrolls' belonged once to their library and, when they were about to fall to the Roman army (it is thought around A.D. 68), they placed their manuscripts for safe keeping in the surrounding caves, where the exceptionally dry atmosphere preserved them astonishingly well over the ensuing nineteen hundred years.

When we visit Qumran, we want to see, first, the monastery ruins and, second, the caves. Nowadays the bus brings us to within a stone's throw of the monastery; a year or two back it was a much more strenuous enterprise, involving a hectic car drive over a bumpy road and a bit of a climb at the end of it.

As we walk round the excavations and try to think ourselves back into the time when these ruins were complete and peopled by the Essene Community, we note that many of the component parts of the structure have been definitely identified—a two-storey defence tower with the basement as a storehouse, cisterns, a kitchen, a refectory, a scriptorium and others.

Having made a circuit of the remains of the Essene Community building, we walk about a hundred yards beyond the ruins to the edge of the plateau. At this point we are looking directly across at Cave 4, separated from us only by a steep and deep ravine. It was in this cave that the majority of the best preserved and most valuable Dead Sea Scrolls were discovered. It has a quite spectacular situation, placed as it is at the edge of the escarpment and with its mouth facing down the length of the Dead Sea.

Entry to the cave used to be allowed but has long been forbidden as too dangerous. In spite of myself I find that I am indulging in a little bit of boasting. After drawing attention to the depth of the ravine and to the sheer drop into it from the cave, I nonchalantly reveal that I once actually stood inside that cave.

My first visit to Qumran—as I later discovered— was on the day after a tourist had fallen while trying to enter the cave. The authorities had immediately closed off the approach by stretching barbed wire across the narrow path leading across the cliff top and a fair distance down the face of the cliff on either side. We knew nothing about the prohibition until we came face to face

with the barbed wire, and seeing our disappointment, our guide
of that time (Ibrahim was his name) offered to lead some of us
round the barbed wire and to the cave. The only condition he
insisted on was that we should promise to go carefully. This
promise was readily given and we proceeded to clamber down
the cliff face with the aid of very carefully placed hand holds on
the wire, round the post at the end and up the other side. This,
we discovered, was only the beginning. Next we had to walk
warily along an extremely narrow ridge and finally shuffle a few
cautious yards down the side of the precipice (this time without
benefit of hand holds) before we dropped through a hole artificially made in the cave roof some years earlier to facilitate
entrance for the archaeologists.

We had, of course, to repeat the feat in the opposite direction
in order to rejoin the others; and the double journey was quite a
nerve-racking experience. We had, however, made our approach
to the cave before we came onto the monastery plateau. When
we did come there and pushed on to the edge of the spur, we saw
now, with rather blood-chilling clarity, just where we had been
and the route we had followed. As we looked across the depth of
the wadi and contemplated the possible outcome of our bravado,
we felt the short hairs bristling on the backs of our necks. But it
was well worth it for the thrill of having stood ankle deep in the
fine soft dust of that world famous cave floor.

On this occasion such bravado is not even contemplated.

Instead, we return to the bus and go off for a 'swim' in the
Dead Sea. To talk of swimming in the Dead Sea is to use the
term loosely. The salt content of the water is so extraordinarily
high that it has a buoyancy that has to be experienced to be
believed. That high salt content also means that it is an extremely
painful thing to allow any of the water to splash into one's eyes
and far from pleasant to have it in or around one's mouth.

The result is that the only 'swimming' that can safely be
attempted is a leisurely and splashless back stroke or an equally
leisurely and splashless breast-stroke. But it must be pointed
out here, too, that 'attempted' is being used loosely. For the
buoyancy thrusts one's legs so high in the water that any kind of
swimming becomes a bit of a farce.

It is, however, a pleasurable farce. Bathing in the Dead Sea is a unique sensation and one not to be missed. Like thousands before us and, no doubt, thousands after us we can hardly stop marvelling aloud at the fact that we are able to do things like sitting in the water—*in* the water, not on the bottom of the sea— and read a book.

The fact that an extended spell under the fresh water shower afterwards is not enough to remove all the salt from our skins does not appreciably diminish our enjoyment, and in any event we will very shortly be heading back to our hotel where a hot bath will put that matter to rights.

Before we leave we take the opportunity to learn a little more about the Dead Sea. The Jordan Valley is an extraordinary rift in the earth's surface and of this the Dead Sea takes up the forty-eight deepest miles with an average breadth of between nine and ten. The surface of the Dead Sea is 1290 feet below sea level, its coast being the lowest spot on the surface of the earth. At its north end, the Dead Sea goes to a depth of 1,300 feet but at its south end it becomes very shallow, only some eight to fourteen feet deep.

The remarkable buoyancy of the Dead Sea is accompanied by a very marked bitterness. Both of these characteristics are due to the same factor, the extremely high chemical content of the water, particularly its salt. The reason for this unique feature is that there is no outlet from the Dead Sea, which is fed by the River Jordan and by several streams but has no way of losing any water except by evaporation. In that particular area, so far below sea level, the amount of evaporation through heat is very considerable and, since the Dead Sea's 'feeders' are peculiarly saline because of the nature of the soil through which they flow, we get here water which is about five times more 'salty' than that of any other sea, some 26% as against a normal 5%.

One consequence is that no fish can exist in its waters. This fact, taken along with the desolation that surrounds it, the wilderness, the salt pans, the sparse vegetation, makes the title of *Dead* Sea seem very fitting.

Despite all this, when the sun shines on it, which is practically all the year round, the waters of the Dead Sea present a most attractive appearance—exceedingly blue and sparkling. The trouble with the Dead Sea is just that which is the trouble with many people—it wants to hold on to everything it gets and refuses to give anything away.

CHAPTER SIX

Round Trip to Masada

Departing at the now almost inevitable time of eight o'clock in the morning, we take the Jericho road once more. As we sweep through Bethany and catch sight of the Wilderness with the Dead Sea glinting in the further distance, the spectacle means all the more to us because we have gone this way before. Past the Inn of the Good Samaritan, past the turn-off to Jericho, down to the north end of the Dead Sea and along the coast road as far as Qumran, we are not travelling a yard of road that we have not already covered.

From Qumran it is all fresh territory. We continue on the road, constructed only three or four years ago, that runs along-side the Dead Sea practically all its length from north to south. A mile or two south of Qumran, we come to Ein Feschka, where a freshwater spring pours itself into the Dead Sea. Here facilities have been set up for bathers and picnickers, not least because it affords the opportunity of Dead Sea bathing and fresh water bathing side by side, the spring waters having been dammed up sufficiently to create a small open-air swimming pool.

Continuing southwards we arrive at Ein Gedi which lies almost midway between the north and south ends of the Sea, a place which is encountered several times in the Old Testament. Its name means 'The Spring of the Wild Goats' and it is an oasis which provides a spectacular green area in the middle of the awful desolation which characterises the environs of the Dead Sea.

A small settlement was founded here in 1949, mainly for political reasons. The southern end of the Dead Sea was in Israel but the north was in Jordan, with the border a short distance north of Ein Gedi. The main purpose of the establishment of the 1949 settlement was to provide some kind of stronghold at what was a strategic point. Nowadays it is a most inviting spot for tourists to make a stop or for Jerusalemites to spend a day off.

The most famous of the Biblical references to Ein Gedi is that which tells of the confrontation between David and Saul (1 Samuel 24). Pursued by Saul and his soldiers, David took refuge in a cave at Ein Gedi and events so fell out that David had Saul at his mercy and let him go free and unharmed.

The spring to which Ein Gedi owes its quite luxuriant fertility begins its descent down the mountainside by splashing over the top in a sparklingly attractive waterfall and is named Ein David, David's Fountain. While some take things easy in the heat at the foot of the hill, the rest of us make the ascent by means of the nature trail that takes us alongside the bed of the stream right up to the waterfall. We are more than happy to sluice our arms and faces in the pool below the waterfall before crossing over to follow the path down the other side of the stream. The way back, being downhill, involves considerably less effort than did the climb. In addition, we have before our eyes a panoramic view of the shining blue waters of the Dead Sea.

This pleasant interlude over, we resume our coach journey and some ten miles further south we come to Masada, our chief port of call for the day. The mountain of Masada is about two miles inland from the shore and stands some 1,700 feet above it. Cut off from the rest of its mountain range by the Brook of Ben-Yair to the south and the Brook of Masada to the north, it stands in striking isolation. Our first view of it, from the road, is most impressive.

The name Masada is a hellenised form of the original Hebrew Metsada or Metsuda, meaning a 'stronghold'. and this place was the locus of a poignantly stirring piece of Jewish history.

On this natural fortress that is Masada, some half-a-mile long and an eighth of a mile broad, a tremendous stronghold was fashioned. Jonathan Maccabeus began it when he built a fortress on the top of this awesome rock thrusting up so spectacularly out of the wilderness beside the Dead Sea. But it was Herod the

Great who was the real creator of the Masada that history came to know so well.

He took refuge in the Masada fortress in 42 B.C. when the Parthians captured Jerusalem; and in 34 B.C. he developed the site in almost incredible fashion. He utilised practically the whole of the plateau area on the top of the cliff to build what amounted to a garrison town. He encircled the plateau with a wall and inside the wall he put everything needed for life to go on—including areas for cultivation, reservoirs for water, store caverns for provisions of various kinds, and a sumptuous palace built on the three natural terraces at the north end of the cliff. It must have been a magnificent creation, involving a fantastic feat of building; even today, nineteen centuries later, its ruins speak eloquently of that magnificence.

When Jerusalem was captured by Titus in A.D. 70, a band of Zealots, the most fanatically nationalistic of all the Jews, took refuge in Masada. Perhaps they thought they would be left alone there in such a remote and forbidding part of the country. But Rome was not in the habit of turning its back on rebellious and troublesome subjects. Under General Silva the Roman army pursued the defiant Zealots to their desert fortress on the cliff and set siege to it.

If the rebels had fled to Masada in the belief that here was the place best suited for making a last stand, events more than confirmed the accuracy of their judgement. For three years they held out against the Roman besiegers. At the end of that time Silva built a ramp on the eastern side of Masada, on top of the promontory that thrust up to within 400 feet of the summit, and used this to bring up a battering ram to the level of the edge of the plateau. With this battering ram the defensive wall was breached. The defenders then built an inner wall made of wood packed with earth. Finding that the blows of the ram only made this inner wall more compact, Silva set it on fire. The fire ran through the whole length of the wall and the Romans retired to their camps for the night while it burned.

In the morning they put up their ladders and prepared for what they confidently expected would be the final, if bloody, assault. But when they burst through the still smouldering fire they met only silence and a mass of corpses. The only living persons in Masada were two women and five children who later emerged from a cave where they had taken refuge.

The women told the story. When the inner wall was set ablaze, Eleazar, the commander of the beleaguered garrison, summoned his men together. 'Our cause is lost' he told them. 'Nothing can now stop the Romans overrunning us tomorrow. Rather than fall into Roman hands, or have our wives and children fall into Roman hands', he pleaded passionately, 'it will be much better to kill them and then to kill ourselves'.

His men were in complete agreement. Each man, after a tearful farewell, slew his own family. Then ten of the men were chosen by lot to kill the others. One of these ten was then similarly selected to kill the nine before finally stabbing himself. The only survivors were these two women who had gone into hiding with their children when the plan was mooted.

On that morning in A.D. 73, nine hundred and sixty people lay dead on the top of Masada, having chosen death rather than captivity.

It is only since 1963 that Masada has been excavated and partially restored. When, consequent upon these excavations, it was first opened up for tourists to visit, it was accessible only on foot—from the east by way of Silva's mighty ramp, from the west by the 'Snake' path, so called because of its serpentine ascent of the cliff. Two miles in length, this footpath was long forgotten and well on the way to total obliteration until it was rediscovered by some young ramblers in 1954. Then it was cleared and restored.

It is still perfectly possible to ascend Masada on foot and a fair number of people, in fact, choose to do so. We opt for the cable-car which nowadays plies beneath the hostel, situated beside the old Roman camps at the foot of the hill on its seaward side, and its arrival platform some two hundred feet from the summit.

Once we are at the top, it is enthusiastically agreed that it would have been well worth making the ascent for the sake of the view, even if there had been nothing else to be gained by it. It really is quite stupendous. On the east the whole length of the Dead Sea sparkles in the bright sunshine, with the grey-brown hills of Moab standing guard all along its further shore. A somewhat dizzy 1,700 feet below us we see the cable-car station and, ever so clearly, the outline of the Roman camps and the siege wall which runs all the way round Masada. The siege wall, or Circumvallation, has a circumference of three miles and along its length the remains of no less than eight Roman camps can be easily discerned, three of which are close by our point of departure up the mountain.

Even on the west, where the drop is so much less in parts because of the natural features and the Roman additions, the outlook across the rugged cliffs and into the deep gorges is scarcely less breathtaking.

Yes, it is certainly worth climbing Masada for the view. But there is much more besides. Before us are some remarkable remains of the small garrison township which once occupied this unique site. It is warm up here, exposed to the full glare of the summer sun, and we do not try to make a close investigation of every ruin.

But we do pay particular attention to some things, such as the storehouses at the northern end which could hold vast quantities of food; the massive cisterns, sight of which helps us to understand the claim that even in that extremely dry area Herod was able to store sufficient water to supply the fortress population for as long a period as ten years; and, most of all, the Palace.

Using the natural contours of the north end of the cliff, Herod had a magnificent three-tier palace constructed which included even a bathing pool. Enough of the colonnades and mosaics survive to enable us to visualise the splendour of the original construction—almost incredible in that desolate environment and on an eminence so difficult of access. As we descend the the steps from the topmost terrace to the bottom, a distance of well over a hundred feet, and then climb back up (much more slowly—with frequent compulsory stops to admire the views and take note of features like Silva's great ramp), we marvel more and more at how such a feat of construction could have been performed in those distant days. But the evidence that it was somehow done is before our eyes.

On our return to the foot of the hill—again by means of the cable car—we file once more into the bus, not for the first time giving thanks for its air-conditioning. A few miles further south, a café on the very shore of the Dead Sea is where we stop to have our picnic lunch. It seems so long and we have seen so much since we left Jerusalem, that it is hard to realise that it is still only very early afternoon. But lunch it is and the place where we eat it, close to the south end of the Dead Sea, is believed to be where the biblical city of Sodom once stood. Not far away is a standing pillar of salt which is pointed out as Lot's wife who, of course, in her flight from the destruction overtaking Sodom and its companion city Gomorrah, 'looked back and became a pillar of salt' (Genesis 19:26).

Lunch taken, we continue on our way. We are not to retrace our route to Jerusalem. Instead, we head still further south, practically to the very end of the Dead Sea coastline, and then we swing off to the right and take the road to Beersheba. Soon the road begins to rise sharply and before long we have some striking views of the patterns, sometimes grotesque, sometimes beautiful, that erosion has carved out in the wilderness hills.

For a short period we continue to see the Dead Sea glinting bright blue beyond the hills to the east, that is, on our right-hand side. When it passes completely from our sight, the sheer desolation of the countryside seems all at once to become doubly severe. We skirt the eastern edge of the Sinai desert and pass within close distance of Beersheba, capital of the Negev.

Despite the interest and importance of ancient Beersheba in Old Testament times, particularly with relation to the Patriarchs, we have not time to visit it. We have to be content with a view of it from the highway as we proceed on our way towards Hebron, thirty-two miles to the north, where we make our next stop.

Hebron lies some ten miles south of Bethlehem and it, too, features prominently in the Old Testament. One of the most

Plate 9.   The Garden of Gethsemane and the Church of All Nations
(*pages* 28-29)

Plate 10.   Northern Palace, Masada (*page* 43)

Courtesy Israel Government Tourist Office

Plate 11.   The Pool of Siloam and Hezekiah's Tunnel (*page* 47)

Plate 12. The Wailing Wall (*page 50*)

Plate 13.   The Dome of the Rock (*page 52*)

ancient cities in the world, it made its first appearance in history when Abraham purchased the Cave of Machpelah for the burial of his wife Sarah. That same Cave of Machpelah is the centre-piece of Hebron today. In time it became the burial place of Abraham as well as of Sarah: and also of two other couples, Isaac and Rebecca, and Jacob and Leah. Over the cave now stands a Moslem mosque surrounded by a wall, and the spot is very sacred to both Jews and Moslems. This is a potential source of discord in a Moslem town now administered by an Israeli government.

We take time in Hebron to visit three places: the Mosque, obviously, containing the six large cenotaphs which are reputed to stand directly over the remains of the patriarchs, a glass factory (for Hebron is famous for a glass-blowing industry that goes back into the mists of time, some say to the time of David who reigned in Hebron for seven and a half years before capturing Jerusalem and making it his capital) and a pottery where we cannot help being reminded of Jeremiah watching the potter at work long ago, as we look on at the modern potter practising what are the self-same skills even though he has the advantage of an electrically driven wheel.

We take note as we drive out of Hebron that this is a very fertile region. It is in fact a notable fruit-growing district.

It has been a long day but this does not prevent our taking time to turn a little off the road before we come to Bethlehem in order to look at Solomon's Pools. These are three reservoirs whose origin is attributed to King Solomon but which certainly owe their present form to Pontius Pilate. He constructed them as a water supply for Jerusalem, piping it to the Holy City through Bethlehem. The Pools look quite lovely, reflecting the overhanging trees in the late afternoon sunshine, and provide a pleasing finish to the day's sightseeing activities.

CHAPTER SEVEN

In and Around the Old City

We think it advisable not to journey far afield the following day, after the fairly strenuous Masada trip. As a result we spend the whole day visiting places in and around the Old City.

Our first visit is to the Church of St. Peter en Gallicantu (St. Peter of the Cock Crow) which faces our hotel on the other side of the Kedron Valley. Built on what is claimed to be the site of the palace of Caiaphas, the high priest at the time of Jesus's death, it is a striking building both outside and in.

We are greeted by one of the French Assumptionist Fathers whose church this is. With the aid of a map affixed to the inside of the door, he explains (as had Sister Agnes of the Ecce Homo Convent) how the walls of Jerusalem have undergone change upon change in the course of the centuries. Although inside the present city walls, Calvary was outside the city as it was at the time of the Crucifixion; while the site on which we stand, now outside the city, was then inside it.

Now we enter the church and are arrested, and not a little moved, by the beautiful modern mosaics which run all round the walls and tell the story of Jesus before Caiaphas and of Peter's denial of his Lord. We learn that all of this mosaic work was the labour of one priest. Then our escort takes us below the church to show us the fascinating remains of what many believe were in fact the paraphernalia of Caiaphas's palace—notably the bottle-necked dungeon and its overlooking guardroom. This guardroom has a window overseeing the dungeon below and a step projecting from the wall to enable the guard to hoist himself up and look down into it.

In the guardroom our Assumptionist guide points out holes in the stone pillars, used, he says, to fasten the prisoners' hands and feet when they were to be flogged. He indicates also the bowls

46

gouged out of the floor which contained salt and vinegar, used either to make the whip more vindictive or to disinfect the wounds it caused—or both.

When we all troop down the steps and crowd into the bottle dungeon, we read, at the priest's request, from Psalm 88: '. . . I am counted with them that go down into the pit . . . thou hast laid me in the lowest pit, in darkness—shall thy wonders be known in the dark'? Our escort now switches out the light and we stand for a few moments in the near dark and try to visualise a little of what it must have been like to be imprisoned in a dungeon of this sort in total blackness. Jeremiah, we know, suffered such a fate; and the Assumptionist Fathers think that Jesus may have been lodged in this very cell prior to the final act of the drama of his passion.

Leaving the church, we take the ancient Roman steps that we saw earlier from the balcony and make our way down in the direction of the Pool of Siloam. Some are very disappointed, even shocked, when we actually arrive at Siloam. Certainly it is not a very prepossessing sight. Walled in nowadays and reached only by descending a flight of stone steps, the Pool is quite busy when we reach it. Emerging from a tunnel, it is a rough rectangle of water almost two feet in depth which at the moment is the scene of women collecting water to carry home for domestic use and also of children bathing. Whatever it may have been in the time of Jesus, the Pool of Siloam is not the prettiest of sights today. Its story, however is one of the most fascinating to be heard in this fascinating land.

It goes back to 701 B.C. when Hezekiah was King in Jerusalem and the Assyrians were threatening to besiege the city. It was a matter of grave concern to Hezekiah in those circumstances of imminent siege that the city was dependent for its water on a single spring, the Gihon ('gushing'), located outside the city walls. He decided that the city's water supply must be safe-guarded if there were to be any hope of resisting the siege. Accordingly, he set his engineers to work in great haste at cutting a tunnel that would run underground from the Gihon to what is now the Pool of Siloam.

The successful execution of Hezekiah's plan was surely one of the most remarkable engineering feats of ancient times. Two squads set to work with their axes and their picks at either end of the proposed tunnel, one at Gihon and the other at Siloam, with the intention of linking up in the middle—and this, remember, was as far back in the past as 701 B.C. Despite the need for speed—the axe and pick marks on the tunnel walls indicate plainly the frenzied hurry of the operation—and despite all that they lacked in terms of modern engineering expertise and equipment, Hezekiah's engineers managed to meet in the middle of the tunnel as planned.

True, the tunnel winds a bit so that there are 1,749 feet of it (533 metres) although a straight line from Gihon to Siloam measures only 1,098 feet. It has not yet been established what was the reason for the somewhat circuitous route followed. True, too, there are places where the men boring the tunnel seem to have lost direction for a brief interval, cutting the wrong way for a foot or two before getting back to the correct line. In the end, however, they joined up together.

The Bible references to this stupendous undertaking are 1 Kings 1: 45 and 2 Kings 20: 20. An inscription in Hebrew, engraved on the tunnel wall near its outlet into Siloam, also commemorates the feat. Accidentally discovered in 1880, it speaks of the two groups of workmen breaking through to each other, guided by the sound of their voices and of their tools. This inscription has been removed from the tunnel and is now preserved in the Museum of the Ancient Orient at Istanbul.

It is still possible to walk the whole length of this Tunnel of Hezekiah, and some of us are keen to do so. While the others wait at the Pool of Siloam, we make our way along the Kedron Valley to Gihon (known better nowadays as the 'Virgin's Fountain') for we are to start from this end. We have been warned that in parts the water may reach waist high. Accordingly we are all well prepared for the adventure, with swimming trunks, bathing suits, shorts and, not least important, bathing shoes.

Armed with our torches, we pick our way down the steps,

very carefully as we near the bottom for here the steps are wet and slippery. We edge through a little gap and step down into a not very large pool. This makes us catch our breath for, by contrast with the heat of the day we have just left, the water that clutches at us seems quite chill—and reaches rather farther up our legs than we had really expected.

Across the pool we see an opening. This is the beginning of the tunnel and the beginning also, of a thrilling and, sometimes even moving, thirty-minutes stroll of a most unusual kind. Sometimes we are able to stand fully upright; most of the time we have to walk with a forward stoop; occasionally we are almost bent double as we wade slowly along the third of a mile of the tunnel's length. This is because the height of the tunnel varies considerably from one point to another. What is more, the variations often come suddenly and unexpectedly so that time and again we are very glad that we have our torches in our hands. Without them our heads would frequently make painful contact with the tunnel roof.

Our debt to our torches does not end there. Their light not only enables us to see our way and to avoid knocking ourselves against the rock, it also allows us to see the fascinating sight of the marks left on the tunnel walls and roof by the tools used to cut the passage. Nearly three thousand years ago it may have been but they look so fresh that they might have been made only yesterday.

There is no lack of food for thought as we splash our way gently and slowly along the winding length of the tunnel—in the single file that its narrowness makes necessary—until the appearance of a circle of light ahead indicates that we are in sight of the tunnel's other end. Soon we are blinking our way back into the bright sunshine and the Pool of Siloam.

*   *   *

The afternoon of the same day also escorts us far back into Jerusalem's past as we visit the 'Temple Area', that part of the

Old City where once stood the Temple of Solomon. But on the way we are brought face to face with history of a much more modern vintage.

Taxis transport us to the Dung Gate, one of the seven entrances to the Old City and so called because in ancient times it was through here that the refuse of the city was taken and deposited in the valley below. From the Dung Gate we can see the Wailing Wall only some few hundred yards away. The bottom two layers of huge stone blocks which make up this Wall, beyond which lies the Temple Area and which is also referred to as the Western Wall, are believed by many Jews actually to date back to Solomon's Temple.

This wall is held in great veneration by the Jews and every day vast numbers of them come here to say their prayers and recite the scriptures. The area immediately in front of the Wall is roped off and is divided into two sections, one for men and one for women, because Jewish men and women do not join together for worship. The worshippers stand facing the Wall, often rocking back and forwards on their heels as they pray— and frequently pressing into the cracks and crevices scraps of paper bearing written prayers.

It is here—even if the first-time pilgrim may not be immediately aware of it—that we are confronted with very recent history. Because of their great veneration for it, one of the features that the Jews found most distressing in the Palestine partition settlement of 1948 was that they were denied access to the Wailing Wall.

For nineteen years no Jew was able to say his prayers before these sacred stones. This meant that when the Six Days' War took place in 1967 and when the Israeli Army captured the Old City on 7 June of that year, not one soldier in that army had been within sight of the Wailing Wall for all of that time, and many of the younger men had never been there at all.

It was little wonder that their joy was so unbounded that, once the Dung Gate was stormed, some of the soldiers threw caution aside and rushed to the Wall even while the bullets were still flying. Nor was it very surprising that the densely populated area between the Wall and the Dung Gate should be quickly cleared.

The last bullet had scarcely been fired that evening when a loud-hailer informed the inhabitants that this section of the city, about a quarter of a mile square, was to be evacuated at once. The whole area was to be bulldozed flat; the mass of houses cheek by jowl with each other and the intricate maze of lanes and alleys running through them were all to be consigned to oblivion; and the process was to start in a few hours time.

Four hours later the work of demolition began; and the clearance has left the Wailing Wall standing in strikingly unobstructed splendour. As we approach it, we find that the concourse immediately before the Wall is thronged with people, including parties of schoolchildren. Most of us move up close to the Wall, the men first putting on one of the little black skull caps made available for the purpose and the women making sure that their arms are covered.

As we stand there amongst a people at prayer at one of their most sacred sites, it is not difficult to sense something of what these blocks of stone mean to them. 'Wailing' Wall is how it is termed and it symbolises the sorrow of Israel as its people gather here to lament for their nation's sins and troubles. Some of us think of the legend which declares that the drops of dew which cover the stones at night are the tears shed by the Wall as it weeps with all Israel.

The Wailing Wall is nowadays one of the Walls enclosing the Temple Area and that is what we make for next. As the name indicates, this is the part of Old Jerusalem which was occupied in ancient times by the Temple of Solomon. Today on that spot stands the Mohammedan 'Dome of the Rock', sometimes but mistakenly referred to as the Mosque of Omar.

As we approach the entrance to the Temple Area, to the side of the Wailing Wall and above the prayer concourse, everything we are carrying is given a security examination before the soldiers on duty wave us through. Once inside the Temple Area our first reaction is one of rather awed surprise. The sheer size of the area is far beyond what any first-time visitor expects.

This is perhaps because most of us grow up with the idea of the Temple as something after the size and shape of one of our churches. In fact, while the Holy of Holies, at the centre of it all, was relatively small, the Temple and its environs covered an enormous area—roughly speaking that very area now before our eyes, approximately 34 acres in extent.

Dominating the scene—as, indeed, it tends to dominate every view of the Old City—is the majestic Dome of the Rock. This is an exceedingly beautiful building and, as we shall shortly discover, it is even more beautiful inside than out. Its Arabic name is Haram es-Sharif ('Noble Sanctuary') and it is second only to Mecca in the Mohammedan world.

The Dome of the Rock goes back to the seventh century. Building was begun in A.D. 685 and completed in A.D. 691. Like most ancient buildings in the Holy Land it has suffered a number of vicissitudes with the passing centuries. Its dome, for instance, although it still reflects golden fire from the sun's rays, is no longer covered with real gold as in the beginning. Now it is covered with gold-plated aluminium; but the beauty of that golden coloured dome surmounting exquisite mosaics is surely no less today than ever it was.

A number of places in the Holy Land are sacred to Christian, Jew and Muslim alike. This is one. The Dome of the Rock is built round the rock-top of Mount Moriah, the spot where, in obedience to what he believed to be the Lord's will, Abraham was prepared to sacrifice his son Isaac (Genesis 22:2). It was here, on Mount Moriah, that King Solomon erected the First Temple, completed in 960 B.C. and destroyed by the Babylonians in 587 B.C. Its rebuilding to form the Second Temple was completed about 520 B.C.

The Second Temple shared in the ups and downs of Jewish history over the following centuries and was showing the effects when Herod the Great decided on a massive plan of rebuilding. It was in 17 B.C., after much careful preparation, that he commenced the actual building of the splendid new Temple that was still under construction in Jesus's day. Herod's Temple was not completed until A.D. 62 and only eight years later it was totally destroyed by the Romans under Titus.

It is on the same site, over the same sacred rock, that there stands now the beautiful Moslem edifice that we call the Dome of the Rock. Before we approach it, standing impressively clear in the middle of the enormous space that is the Temple Area, we visit another large building on its southern side. This is the Mosque of El Aqsa. While the Dome of the Rock is today no more than a sacred showpiece, El Aqsa is still a place of regular worship.

Although not able to rival the Dome of the Rock, it has its own attractiveness inside as we see for ourselves when, following the requirements rigidly enforced, we slip off our shoes and enter in our stockinged feet. El Aqsa, too, has its history, grim and recent. This was the building damaged seriously just a few years ago when a visiting Australian started a fire in an apparent outburst of religious mania; and it was here that King Abdullah was assassinated in 1951.

From El Aqsa Mosque we make our way to the Dome of the Rock, passing a place for ablutions, where Mohammedans wash before entering the mosque to say their prayers. As we come closer we are struck even more by the sheer beauty of this Moslem shrine; when we go inside, again leaving our shoes at the door, we find ourselves in an interior whose lush carpets, magnificent windows and splendid cupola make its superb loveliness a match for the exterior that we admired so much.

We leave the Temple Area by a different gate. This takes us out on to the Via Dolorosa and we make our way past the Ecce Homo Convent in the direction of St. Stephen's Gate. Just short of that Gate we turn aside into the grounds of St. Anne's Church.

The Church of St. Anne, built over the traditional site of the birthplace of Mary, mother of Jesus, is a Crusader Church and most impressive in its severe simplicity. Its façade was badly damaged in the 1967 war but has now been completely restored.

Close by the church is the Pool of Bethesda. We have often to remind ourselves in Jerusalem that the present-day city, resting as it does upon the wreckage and debris of violent centuries, stands high above the ground level of ancient times. At the Pool of Bethesda our eyes, rather than our imaginations, inform us of this fact. The incomplete excavations have uncovered, far below, steps leading down to the remnants of that pool which was the scene of one of Jesus's healing miracles (John 5: 1-9). To descend these steps, with the large slice of visible history carved out of the earth around them, is like taking a gigantic stride back across nineteen and a half centuries. We find the experience romantic and impressive even though what remains for us to see today is no more than a little pool of near-stagnant water. We find it challenging, too, as we gather together again for a few moments outside the church to read John's narrative and hear again that question of Jesus which is often so crucial, 'Do you really want to be made whole'?

From the Church of St. Anne, it is only a few steps to St. Stephen's Gate and the end of the day's pilgrimage. It was from this exit—or at least its predecessor of the time, so tradition has it—that Stephen was hustled to his martyrdom (Acts 7: 57-60). It is also known as the Lions' Gate because of the two pairs of lions carved in the stone above the entrance. Just along from St. Stephen's Gate, close up against the city wall, are the graves of many Arabs, buried there so that they may be close to the Holy City on the Day of Judgement. From this burial place we obtain a splendid view of the Mount of Olives on the opposite side of the Kedron Valley from where we stand.

The sweep of this famous slope, as it descends majestically from the Church of the Ascension to the Garden of Gethsemane, plucks at our heart-strings once more as its profound Christian associations come crowding in upon us.

CHAPTER EIGHT

Round and About

Our time in Jerusalem is fast running out, but there is still a great deal not yet seen and, of course, there is still a lot of shopping to be done. The next day, therefore, is spent in the immediate and not quite so immediate environs of the Old City.

We start off very close to it, underneath it in fact, and pay a visit to Solomon's Quarries. Discovered accidentally more than a hundred years ago by a man walking with his dog round the walls of Jerusalem, King Solomon's Quarries are a gigantic cavern that extends more than 200 yards beneath the streets of the Old City.

The entrance is located in the city wall midway between Damascus Gate and Herod's Gate. As soon as we enter we feel we are in a totally different world. In contrast to the bright, hot sunshine that we have left, the interior of the cavern is cool and dimly lit. More than that, our imaginations transport us swiftly across the bridge of many centuries.

It was here, so it is said, that the stones were quarried to build Solomon's Temple. As we walk round the massive vault, with its white walls still showing clearly the marks of the ancient stone-cutters, we cannot help thinking of the vivid account of that building in 1 Kings 5 and 2 Chronicles 2.

There are rocks and stones strewn about in great profusion on the cavern floor, among them chips no doubt left by those masons of long ago. Some pick up pieces as souvenirs—for a fragment of white stone from Solomon's Quarries makes a particularly pleasing take-home memento for a Freemason friend. Masons hold Solomon's Quarries in particular regard because they believe that the builders of the Temple were the first Freemasons; such pieces of stone, shaped into the form of masonic insignia, find their way right across the world.

From Solomon's Quarries we go round the walls of the Old City, past Damascus Gate, New Gate, Jaffa Gate, Zion Gate and on to Mount Zion. Here there is much to see, for here, directly across the Valley of Hinnom (Gehenna) from St. Andrew's Church of Scotland, are the Tomb of David, the Holocaust, the Church of the Dormition and the Cenacle.

It is not now generally thought that King David is actually buried on Mount Zion. But for many centuries it was believed that he was and this place is still venerated as his burial place by the Jews. The Tomb of King David is, in fact, one of the most sacred of all Jewish sites.

Above the Tomb of King David is the large bare room known as the Cenacle, the traditional site of the Room of the Last Supper. It is reached from King David's Tomb by coming out into the open, going through a narrow door in the side of the wall, across some old cobbles and up a flight of steep steps.

'Cenacle' is derived from the Latin Coenaculum which means 'dining-hall'. The room as it is today is devoid of any furnishing but wears for all to see the trappings of its varied history. In its time it has been part of a Franciscan monastery and also, for a long period, a place of Mohammedan worship. It cannot, of course, be the actual room in which the Last Supper took place, but Christian tradition has long held that it was on this site, or at least very close to the spot, that the original Upper Room once stood. In any event, for us, again trying to see the holy thing behind the holy place, it is a memorable experience just to be there and to read together the story of how the Sacrament of the Lord's Supper was begun.

Next we visit the Church of the Dormition not far away. The Latins believe it is built on the spot where Mary, mother of Jesus, died or 'fell asleep', hence the title 'Dormition' (from the Latin verb dormire, meaning 'to fall asleep'). In the upper church a golden mosaic above the altar depicts Mary with the infant Jesus. On the tiled floor is a striking representation of the signs of the Zodiac, along with other symbols, the names of prophets and saints and a quotation from Proverbs 8: 23.

In the crypt is what most Roman Catholic pilgrims partic-

ularly want to see—a life-size marble figure of the virgin on her
death-bed, lying beneath a cupola in the centre of which Jesus is
depicted as calling his mother to heaven. The effigy of Mary is
placed in the centre of the crypt and round the walls is a series of
beautiful little chapels donated by various countries, their
mosaic representations speaking markedly of their place of
origin.

Also on Mount Zion and close by King David's Tomb is the
Chamber of the Martyrs. This, with its accompanying in-
scribed stone standing outside, is a memorial to the millions of
Jews who died in the holocaust of Nazi Germany.

We leave Mount Zion and head for the New City. As we are
on a Christian pilgrimage, our tour inevitably concentrates on
the places associated with the life of Jesus. The walled city of
Old Jerusalem is, therefore, what must command most of our
interest in a short stay. But as we took time to look back to
something of Israel's past in our visit to Masada, so we take time
to catch a glimpse, brief though it has to be, of her present.

New Jerusalem is not nowadays physically separated from Old
Jerusalem. Between 1948 and 1967 they were set apart by walls
and barriers, by no-man's land and by the Mandlebaum Gate.
Today the one simply begins where the other comes to an end.
When we come in our bus up from the Kedron Valley and
alongside the North Wall of the Old City, we pass by Herod's
Gate, Damascus Gate and New Gate, and then go through a
set of traffic lights. Once through these lights, we are already in
New Jerusalem. Today we leave Mount Zion and drive along
the west wall of the Old City past Jaffa Gate to the same set of
traffic lights.

The New City has a population of well over 200,000 which
makes it much more populous than Old or Eastern Jerusalem,
including the Walled City, whose total population is about
75,000. The inhabitants of the New City are mostly Jews, those
of the Old City are mostly Arabs.

We have not time to stop at any point in the heart of New
Jerusalem. All we can do is observe as much as possible from the
bus—the busy shopping thoroughfares, the strictly orthodox

Jewish area where on the Sabbath nothing is open, no money is
spent and no work whatever is done, and the residential area.

Now we find ourselves on the campus of the Hebrew University. It is understandably difficult for the first time tourist to
become geographically orientated with regard to the various
places of interest and importance clustered in and around the
Old City. But this is probably nothing to the confusion created in
his mind by the Hebrew University. For it is really in three parts.

The first is on Mount Scopus which rises high above Jerusalem about two miles to the north-east, that is, beyond the
Mount of Olives and on the way north to Samaria. The partition
settlement of 1948 meant that the Jewish area on Mount Scopus,
which included the former Hadassah Hospital as well as the
University, was cut off from Israeli Jerusalem (because the road
leading to it was in Jordan and therefore unusable).

The Israelis, therefore, set about building a new University
on the west side of the New City. It is this new Hebrew University we are now seeing—the replacement for that first University
on Mount Scopus which became inaccessible in 1948. But
Mount Scopus was reunited to Jerusalem with the 1967 War
and a third University campus is being laid out there adjoining
the original.

Close beside the University buildings stands the Israeli
Parliament (the Knesset) and beside it are several other Government offices. The buildings we are looking at—those of the
University and those of the Government—are all of recent
construction. So is the Israeli Museum which is adjacent.

The most striking part of the Israel Museum Compound, and
indeed of the whole area, is the Shrine of the Book. Its shining
white dome, made in the likeness of the lid of a Dead Sea Scroll
jar, stands out most impressively. It was built specifically to
house these famous scrolls and we take time to go in and see
them.

From the Shrine of the Book and the Museum Compound
we continue westwards. We pass close by the modern Hadassah
Hospital whose grounds contain a small synagogue in which are

twelve famous Chagall stained glass windows representing the twelve tribes of Israel.

The village of Ein Karem, birthplace of John the Baptist, lies in the valley below Hadassah and we make the steep descent to visit the Franciscan Church of St. John, built over the place where, so tradition claims, John was born.

For a time we leave the main road and embark on a rather lovely coach tour through some most attractive countryside. The road is narrow and winding but the driving is of high standard and the deviation from the highway makes for a pleasant interlude.

Shortly we arrive at the Arab village of Abu Ghosh. This is considered by some to be the site of the Emmaus which was the locus of a dramatic happening on the first Easter Day (Luke 24: 13-35). It certainly fits in very well with the distance of approximately seven miles which separated Emmaus from Jerusalem (Luke 24: 13).

Abu Ghosh has additional claims on our interest. It stands on the site of the Biblical Kiryat-Yearim where the Ark of the Covenant rested for twenty years (1 Chronicles 13: 5-8). It was also invested by the Crusaders and the remains of their church are among the best preserved Crusader remains in the country.

From the hill-top above the village a splendid view can be obtained of the outskirts of Jerusalem built on the heights. Here the pilgrim journeying from the coast catches his first sight of the Holy City. Perhaps that was why Abu Ghosh came to mean so much to the Crusaders. It certainly makes it more meaningful to us and we are already in a receptive mood when we enter the church and go down into the crypt.

Here a little spring flows through the Crusader remains that have resisted the centuries remarkably well. The acoustics are particularly fine in this place and so we gather round the spring for brief devotions. The reading is a part of the Emmaus Story, including its exultant declaration, 'It is true: the Lord has risen'. Our own feeling of exultation, however, reaches an even higher level when we sing together the twenty-third psalm to the tune Crimond. Few of us have voices that would ever pass any kind of audition but the superb acoustics gather up our singing and swell it into a sound of such splendour that we feel it is likely to echo in our memories for ever.

CHAPTER NINE

Links with Home

Our time in Jerusalem is nearly at an end. The last day is to be left free so that all may spend it in the way that suits them best—shopping, perhaps, or revisiting some place or places that have specially appealed to them.

No official group activity is organised for today except for the evening, after dinner. But, since most of us are from the United Kingdom, a number decide to visit one or two places of particular interest to British tourists.

First of all we make our way up Mount Scopus to visit the British War Cemetery. Here, in orderly rows overlooking Jerusalem, moving because of their very simplicity, are the graves of those British soldiers who lost their lives in the conquest of Jerusalem in the First World War.

Military cemeteries are, sadly, not uncommon. There are thousands of them scattered across the world. But, somehow, we short-term exiles from the British Isles find it singularly moving to walk quietly in the bright Israel sunshine among the last resting places of those fellow-countrymen who many years ago fell in battle in this very area.

Motherland sentiment is also markedly present in our next two visits, particularly for the English amongst us first of all and then for the Scots. From Mount Scopus we travel across the Kedron Valley to the immediate vicinity of the Old City and to St. George's Cathedral. The focal point of the Anglican Church in the Holy Land, St. George's, which dates from 1898, is for all the world just like a parish church transported from England and set down in this foreign land. This impression is greatly heightened when, after spending some time in the church, we inspect the garden of the Archbishop's house. It looks as if it might have been plucked from some English vicarage to be set down in its present environment, and its mass of varied blooms is a picturesque sight.

Next stop is the Scottish Church, St. Andrew's, directly across the Valley of Hinnom from Mount Zion. St. Andrew's is a memorial church. The foundation stone was laid by Lord Allenby in 1927 and the church, with the hospice beside it, was built to commemorate those Scots lads and lassies who died in the Palestine Campaign of the First World War. Who could have foreseen then that less than twenty years later, because of another great war, many service men and women were to know the inspiration and the comfort of that church, and to enjoy the hospitality of that hospice.

All our group—the Scots especially, Scottish Presbyterians most of all—find it a moving experience to come to St. Andrew's.

Perhaps this is due to the magnificence of its situation, looking directly across the Valley to Mount Zion and the Old City and, once one knows where to look, the cross that thrusts skywards from the dome centred above Calvary.

Perhaps it is due to the simplicity of the church, almost austere after the many elaborate sanctuaries that we have visited.

Perhaps it is due to the cool whiteness of the church both inside and outside, for the contrast with the mid-afternoon heat is refreshing.

Perhaps it is due to that expression of Scottish sentiment which has set the Communion Table, itself faced with Iona marble, on a slab of that same material so that whenever the minister dispenses the Sacrament he knows that he is standing upon a part of his native land.

It may well be due in part to any or to all of these; but perhaps for the Scots amongst us it is especially due to this. The pews are nearly all the gifts of Scottish bodies and Scottish Kirks and the names of the donors are inscribed on metal plates affixed to the backs of the seats. To wander among these names— Glasgow, Edinburgh, Cumbrae, Methlick, Linlithgow, and the rest—and to be so far from home and to have seen so many other sights, is to bring a lump to the throat.

As we leave the church and go out once more to the terrace facing the Old City, I cannot help reflecting how fortunate I was to be there once at Easter and at the St. Andrew's dawn service. Those of my group who cared to come—and that included nearly everyone of them—rose at 3.30 on that Easter morning. This was for most of us no great effort as the tolling bells at regular intervals through the night had made sleep difficult for us anyway.

We assembled an hour later on the terrace of St. Andrew's, in darkness which would have been total but for the hand torches which we carried. With other visitors from many parts of the world we settled down on the seats carried out from the hospice and sat down to face across to the Holy City.

As we sat there, we could see nothing at all but we knew, all the same, that we were gazing right at the place where, on the first Easter weekend, Jesus had been crucified. There we waited for the new day to come.

As dawn broke, the rising sun suddenly bathed the Way of Sorrow in a golden light and struck golden fire from the cross thrusting heavenward from the roof of the Holy Sepulchre. At this movingly symbolic moment, the minister of St. Andrew's began our worship with the cry, 'The Lord is risen'.

I do not believe that hearts or voices can ever have responded more eagerly or more confidently, 'The Lord is risen indeed'.

In the evening after dinner we go to a church much different from St. Andrew's. It is the Syrian Church of St. Mark and our purpose is to re-enact in some measure the Maundy Thursday walk, the walk Jesus made on the last night of his earthly life, from the place of the Last Supper to Gethsemane.

We have, of course, already on Mount Zion visited the Cenacle, the commonly accepted location of the Upper Room where the Last Supper took place. This ancient Syrian Church is, however, an alternative site—which some count more probable. It is situated within the Old City, in the Armenian quarter and roughly midway between Jaffa Gate and Dung Gate.

Our purpose is to begin from St. Mark's Church and walk as Jesus did out of the Old City, down the hillside, across the

Kedron and up to the Garden of Gethsemane on the lower slopes of the Mount of Olives. This is a fairly well-known devotional exercise among pilgrimage groups and is usually referred to as the Maundy Thursday Walk or the St. Mark's Walk.

'Walk' though it is, we start off by employing a fleet of taxis to take us by the now familiar road past Gethsemane and round the outside of the Old City to the Jaffa Gate. All on foot once more, with our guide at the front and myself at the rear, we plunge into a seeming maze of narrow streets and find ourselves shortly at St. Mark's Church.

Unpretentious in appearance, St. Mark's has several points of interest over and above the possibility that here once stood the house of John Mark's mother, location of the Last Supper and meeting place of the early Church. It was to this small community that some of the first Dead Sea Scrolls were brought in 1947, to be taken in turn by their bishop and sold in the United States. It is in this church that there hangs a famous painting of Virgin and Child which is traditionally ascribed to St. Luke and is patently very old.

For us tonight, however, chief interest lies in the possible association of this situation with the events of the first Maundy Thursday and in the undoubted fact that, whether the precise site of the Upper Room be here or at the Cenacle, or neither, it is undoubtedly in this vicinity.

The liturgical language of the Church of St. Mark is Old Syriac, fairly close to that Aramaic which was the language of Jesus. The priest kindly reads in that language the narrative of the institution of the Lord's Supper. I read the same passage in English and then we embark on our processional walk—in twos and in silence.

Pilgrim groups on this walk used to go out of the city and then leave the road to follow a path down the hillside to the very foot of the Kedron Valley, cross the brook and make their way up the road on the other side, past the Tomb of Absalom, to the Garden of Gethsemane.

A recent winter landslide at the top of the path rules out this route for us and so once we emerge from the Dung Gate we keep to the road all the way. Even this slightly truncated version of the walk is most impressive—snaking our way in a long line through the labyrinthine, narrow streets, skirting past the flood-lit Wailing Wall, leaving the city by the Dung Gate, dropping deeper and deeper towards the valley floor, stopping now and again at convenient spots for brief devotions.

Our walk culminates at the Garden of Gethsemane. It is past the official closing time but by arrangement with the Superior we are allowed in to complete our pilgrimage walk. Not only that, we are given permission to have our final devotions in the Garden proper, among the olive trees.

This is a rare privilege and one to be greatly cherished. It used to be the order of the day that every visitor was allowed ready access to the Garden, at liberty to walk along its paths and stand under its olive trees. But even visitors to the Holy Land and to holy places can at times be irresponsible, it would seem. So many were taking away stones from the paths, twigs and leaves from the trees, that the Franciscan custodians felt obliged a few years ago to deny admission to the Garden proper. Visitors now merely view its touching loveliness from the other side of the low iron fence that runs alongside the pavement leading from the entrance into the Church of All Nations.

On this occasion, however, the priest unlocks the little gate set in the fence and allows us to stand among the trees and flowers for our reading and prayers. As we read the story of Jesus's agony in the garden and offer a prayer, the events of that first Maundy Thursday seem very real and very close. Although there is only a stone wall between us and the main road with its constant, hurrying, twentieth-century traffic, we can almost think we see the flickering of torches through the branches and hear the mutter of voices borne on the breeze as Judas comes to betray his Master with a kiss.

Here, in the darkness of Gethsemane, practically at the end of our stay in Jerusalem, we feel, perhaps as never before, something of the shadow of that pain that Jesus suffered in order to give men and women like us new hope and new life.

> 'Gethsemane can I forget?
> Or there thy conflict see,
> Thine agony and bloody sweat,
> And not remember thee'?

CHAPTER TEN

The Journey North

The following morning sees us in the bus, all packed up, to be transported to Tiberias where we are to spend our remaining time in the Holy Land. It would, however, be prodigal, profligate even, of our time and transport, to be content simply to be moved from the one place of residence to the other. Consequently, as Jesus did on a famous occasion long ago (John 4), we choose to follow the route to Galilee that will take us through Samaria.

So, then, we head over the shoulder of Mount Scopus, catching a farewell panoramic view of Jerusalem as we pass over the crest of the hill; and a succession of Biblical sites follow one another into our field of vision.

Shortly we pass through the village of Sha'afat built adjacent to the site of ancient Gibeah, the capital city of King Saul. A little further on, after passing Jerusalem airport (Kalandia) on the left, we come, on the same side, to the site of Biblical Mizpah, just before we enter the present-day town of Ramallah.

Only a little distance through Ramallah and to the right of the main road we glimpse the village of Bethel, famous because it was here that Jacob's dream took place (Genesis 28:12-18). We are now travelling through the mountains of Samaria and a further few miles enable us to see on the right the ruins of ancient Shiloh, once the religious centre of the tribes of Israel.

Round the shoulder of the hill beyond Shiloh we come upon a spectacular scene. Far below is the fertile valley of Lebona (sometimes Libbona, nowadays Lebun). It was here there took place that festival of 'catch yourself a wife while she dances' which is recorded in Judges 21:19. The road winds down from the heights in a series of loops which afford a succession of magnificent views.

For a time we continue through the mountain country of Samaria until we reach Nablus, capital of modern Samaria. It lies between Mount Gerizim on the one hand and Mount Ebal on the other and stands on the site of ancient Shechem.

Before we enter the town we call in at Jacob's Well. This is one of the best authenticated of all Bible locations. There is no doubt that it was here, at this very well, that Jesus had the historic encounter with the Samaritan woman that is recorded in chapter 4 of St. John's Gospel. Situated in a pleasant garden, the well is enclosed by a structure covering the remains of the Byzantine church which once stood over it. Two doors, one on either side, each with its flight of stairs, lead down to the well and what may have been the crypt of the early church. The well and its superstructure are surrounded by pillars which were to have been a splendid Greek Orthodox church. Building began in 1913 but had to be suspended in 1914 owing to lack of funds and nothing has been done to the project since.

When we descend the steps to the well we find that the old Byzantine crypt has been converted into a little Greek Orthodox chapel, used for daily services. The well itself is surrounded by a low stone parapet and as we gather round, taking it in turns to look down, we see that it is very deep. It is in fact more than a hundred feet deep and when we lower a bucket by means of the windlass and rope attached to the parapet, it takes a considerable time to reach the water and by then it looks little larger than a silver thimble.

When the bucket is hauled back to the top, we each drink some of the cool, clear water, appreciating as we do so that it is drawn from the very same well that provided Jesus with just such a refreshing drink long ago. The bucket is lowered and raised more than once before everyone has had a drink and, in many cases, filled the little water pots which are on sale at the tiny kiosk managed by the priest in the corner.

When all are satisfied, the water left in the bucket is tipped into the well mouth to fall straight down without striking the sides. It takes a long, long time before we hear it splash into the surface of the well water far below.

Plate 14. Mount Zion from St. Andrew's Church (*page 56*)

Plate 15. St. Andrew's Church (*page* 62)

Plate 16. Jacob's Well, Nablus (*page 68*)

Plate 17. Samaritans with the Pentateuch (*page* 69)

Plate 18. The Garden of the Church of the Beatitudes ((*page* 75)

Back in the bus we drive into Nablus, populated almost entirely by Moslem Arabs and the scene of much bitter fighting in the 1967 war. A good way through the town and on that part of it built on the lower slopes of Mount Gerizim, we locate the Samaritan synagogue.

The Samaritan Community is very small, little more than five hundred in the whole country, some four hundred of whom are here in Nablus and the rest in Holon, near Tel-Aviv. We come face to face with one of the ironies of history here. The Samaritans fell foul of the Jews after the exile because they had intermarried with foreigners. Now their numbers have fallen so low that they are in real danger of becoming extinct; and this is largely due to the inbreeding occasioned by a rigid exclusiveness which steadfastly refuses to countenance marriage outside their own sect.

The Samaritan synagogue is a fairly new building which, they are eager to tell us, was built for them by the British to replace one that was fast decaying. When we arrive, the door is closed but a boy appears almost at once to tell us that he will fetch the priests. The door has three locks and the key for each is in the custody of a different member of the hierarchy so that all three must be summoned before we can be admitted.

This takes only a short time, however, as the synagogue is set in the middle of the Samaritan Community. Once we are inside the synagogue, one of the priests tells us a little about his people and, in particular, their veneration for Mount Gerizim on whose peak they camp out for the whole period of the Passover Feast.

Next comes what is for us the highlight of our visit. The priest solemnly brings out for our inspection what he tells us is the oldest book in the world. It is a parchment copy of the Pentateuch, the first five books of the Bible, extremely old and extremely valuable. They once were offered more than a million dollars for it.

Knowing how precious a document this is, I can never avoid feeling that the Samaritans should handle it a bit more carefully than they do. Perhaps they are really more careful than appears to me; but today again I watch with some apprehension as the priest takes the scroll out of its silver case and, with apparently careless nonchalance, unrolls the parchment, now creased and frayed with age, for all of us to see.

The Pentateuch is all that the Samaritans regard as Scripture. This is their whole Bible, and this particular copy is written in the Samaritan script, which is similar to ancient Hebrew. Few people, apart from the Samaritans themselves, are likely to attach much weight to their claim that this was written by Aaron. It is, however, unquestionably very old; and just to look on it there in Nablus, held stretched out in front of him by the Samaritan priest, is to feel oneself stepping backwards through many centuries of time.

Some nine miles north of Nablus, we turn off the highway and climb a steep hillside to the ruins of ancient Samaria, now known as Sebaste. Here we have our picnic lunch, carefully carried with us from Jerusalem. First, however, those whose energy matches their thirst for further sightseeing stroll round the ruins excavated on the very hill top, above the cafe beside which the bus has parked.

It was here that Omri, King of Israel, decided to build his capital city. This was because of its magnificent strategic position, on a high hill that overlooked the surrounding plain on all sides. The date was 887 B.C. Omri's successor, Ahab, added to the buildings. Later, after many changes of fortune, the city was completely destroyed but a new city was built by Herod the Great in 35 B.C., which he called Sebastia in honour of the Roman Emperor Augustus, Sebastos being the Greek form of his name. Some think that it was here that Salome danced her notorious dance for John the Baptist's head. Most scholars reckon, however, that this event was more likely to have taken place in Machaerus, as Josephus indicates.

As we walk round we see excavated remains of all of these foundations, including the palaces of Omri and Ahab and a Roman theatre.

Lunch taken, we head—still northwards—for another dose of ancient history in the shape of Megiddo.

When we leave the mountains of Samaria behind us, we find

ourselves in the Valley of Jezreel, otherwise known as the Plain of Esdraelon. It is the largest valley in Israel and the most fertile area of the country. Its chief town is Afula and some seven miles from Afula is the Tel of Megiddo, standing close to the main road from Haifa. Here have been excavated some interesting remains of one of the world's most ancient cities.

Megiddo is mentioned as far back in history as 1478 B.C. It was attacked in that year by Thutmose III, Pharaoh of Egypt, and the battle is described on the walls of his temple in Upper Egypt. Because of its strategic situation, Megiddo has featured in many military operations since then and its frequent such involvement made it a symbol of war. When the Book of Revelation looks ahead to the final battle that will bring this world to an end, it sees it as taking place at Megiddo—'the place called in Hebrew Armageddon', that is, 'Har Mageddon' or 'the hill of Megiddo' (Revelation 16:14, 16).

Every time I come to an excavated site in the Holy Land, I cannot help saying to myself 'How much more there must be still to uncover if only time and money permitted'. So it is at Megiddo. And yet what has been unearthed is fascinating and my group members find it so as they walk round the site with me.

As we walk, we learn that it was here that King Josiah fell in battle against the Pharaoh in 610 B.C. (2 Chronicles 28:20). We hear, too, that previously King Solomon had fortified the city (Kings 9:15). From the top of the mound, we see a marvellous view of the Valley of Jezreel, with Mount Tabor and Nazareth in the background. Of the actual excavations, there is particular interest in seeing the remains of a Canaanite Temple which is to be dated about 1900 B.C. and which contains a remarkably well preserved altar; a large silo equally well preserved, with two flights of steps running diagonally all the way from top to bottom; and the place where a section of the hillside has been sheared off, for all the world like cutting a slice of cake, to reveal at a glance the distinctive marks of ten or eleven civilisations.

Perhaps most fascinating of all is our exit from the site. For Megiddo, like Jerusalem, can boast of an underground water tunnel artificially constructed to ensure that in time of siege the city's water supply would be safe. The two constructions are scarcely to be compared except in terms of their purpose but each is remarkable in its own way.

The Water Tunnel, situated at the southern end of the Tel, is cut through the rock of the hillside at a depth of about 200 feet. To get to it we have to descend—quite steeply—nearly 200 steps. Unlike Hezekiah's this tunnel is not a water course; it was cut as a means of subterranean approach to the spring. We are, therefore, able to walk dry shod—and upright—along its 400 feet length. When we climb the rather fewer steps at the other end, we find to our relief that the bus is waiting to collect us as arranged.

We rejoin the main road just a short distance away and head for Tiberias. Tiberias, the capital of Galilee, lies on the shore of the Sea of Galilee. It is 682 feet below sea level and is hot in summer, warm in winter; and is almost 2,000 years old. Herod Antipas erected a new town here in A.D. 20 on the ruins of an old one and named it in honour of the Emperor Tiberius. Tiberias has undergone many ups and downs since then but today it is a thriving and steadily expanding town that is almost entirely Jewish.

Passing through Afula and round the base of Mount Tabor we press eastwards towards Tiberias, following the fine modern road, with its avenue of eucalyptus trees on either hand, that in its turn follows more or less the old Via Maris, the sea route, the caravan way from the coast in ancient times.

Suddenly we sweep round a slight bend and all at once the Sea of Galilee lies spread out below us. To come upon it like this, even though I am looking out for it, never fails to recapture for me something of the thrill of awed delight I felt when this sight first burst upon my view. The lake is so beautiful, with its exquisite shade of blue highlighted by the afternoon sun.

I am not the only one to catch my breath. For this little stretch of water is very lovely indeed and for Christians, of course, full of associations with their Lord. The Sea of Galilee has several names—Lake Galilee, Sea of Tiberias, Gennesaret, for instance.

The Israelis frequently call it Lake Kinneret which literally means 'like a harp' (a 'harp' in Hebrew is 'Kinner'). This name is variously explained as due to the fact that the lapping of its waves on the shore makes a sound as pleasant as the music of a harp or to the fact that its shape is like that of a harp.

The Sea of Galilee is 13 miles long and its greatest width is 9 miles. It is $32^1/_2$ miles in circumference and at its deepest it is about 160 feet. Tiberias is situated about halfway along the lake on its western shore. Towering over the lake on its eastern side are the hills which, prior to 1967, were Syrian but are now in Israeli hands. Beyond them and to the north rise the Golan Heights; and from our present position on a clear day snow-capped Mount Hermon can be seen standing majestic sentinel behind the Golan.

Today it is too hazy and Hermon is wrapped away from our sight. But the rest of the scene is there to be etched on the memory for ever. It has been said that the Hebrew name of the town, Teveriya, was formed by the contraction of two Hebrew words Tov Reiya meaning 'lovely in view'. As we drink in the scene, this explanation seems thoroughly plausible.

Although Tiberias was first established on the very shores of the sea, in recent years it has been steadily pushing up the hillside until now the new building has reached the very top of the hill. We, however, are to be staying in the old part of the town, in the Church of Scotland Hospice, at the very foot, beside the sea.

As the road rapidly descends and we get nearer to the sea, we notice a change in the character of the buildings. Many of these in the older part of Tiberias are built of black basalt, a volcanic rock common in the region.

The bus deposits us at the archway leading into the Scots Hospice, our home for the next week. The Church of Scotland presence has been in Tiberias for more than a century and the building before us now was originally a missionary hospital. When, after the partition of 1948, Israel decided to take all medical work into its own hands, the Church of Scotland converted its hospital into a hospice for pilgrims such as us.

CHAPTER ELEVEN

Around the Lake

There is nothing in Tiberias itself of Biblical significance, but there is a very great deal on the lake on which it stands and around its shores, particularly to the north.

On the first day at Tiberias we make a bus tour of the north end of the lake. From the gate of the hospice, the road north runs right alongside the sea for several miles. As we go we see on our left the Horns of Hattin, where Saladin led the Saracens to victory in their last and decisive battle against the crusaders in A.D. 1187. We see, too, a little way further along, the small Christian burial place, scraped out of the hillside, which commands a touchingly lovely view across the Sea of Galilee. On a previous visit, one of my pilgrims—himself on his second tour—died suddenly in Tiberias. His wife was also with us—and by her wish we buried him there, overlooking a scene which he had come to love.

As we continue on our way we take note of the many crops being cultivated, notably bananas, and observe also the water being piped from Lake Galilee on the way south to irrigate the Negev. This latter policy has occasioned much controversy. Many who live in the vicinity of the lake are fearful of its future if this 'stealing' of its waters is to continue. The level, they say, has already dropped to a threatening extent.

After passing the traditional site of the Magdala of New Testament times, just a huddle of stones today, the road ceases to hug the lakeside so closely, turns slightly inland and rises abruptly. In a few moments we see through a grove of trees the Church of the Beatitudes, poised on a hilltop, and shortly afterwards we arrive at its gates.

Tradition has it that it was at this spot, or hereabouts at least, that Jesus preached his Sermon on the Mount and, in particular, uttered the Beatitudes (Matthew 5:1-10). The church and hospice which now stand here were built in 1937 by an Italian Franciscan order of nuns. The hospice stands on the very crest of the hill and the church a little lower down nearer to the lake. The black-domed church is not large and is more attractive in appearance inside than out, with its gold mosaic dome, the ceiling bearing the Beatitudes inscribed in Latin, and its pavement around the altar carrying representations of the seven virtues.

When we move out of the church into the cloisters that encircle it, we come upon a scene that grips the heart. We look along the length of the Sea of Galilee from high above its waters. As the sea, blue and still, sparkles in the bright sunlight, we recall that these very slopes rolling below us to its edge, empty of people at the moment, used often to see thousands gather to hear Jesus preach.

While our group lingers round the church, I go into a corner of the grounds that lie between hospice and church. I have already sought and obtained permission from one of the Italian Sisters—always readily given—to hold a Communion Service there. Once preparations are complete, the group gather together under the trees, using the low walls as pews, and we celebrate the Sacrament of the Lord's Supper. We celebrate after the form of the Church of Scotland, with two of the group acting as assisting elders, but the invitation to 'partake' is given to all irrespective of denomination.

Perhaps nothing has been more moving or inspiring for us than this. Here on the Mount of Beatitudes, with that Sea of Galilee which Jesus knew so well before our eyes and with the increasing chorus of the birds sounding in our ears, for all the world like some heavenly choir, we feel our Lord's presence very near as we eat the broken bread and drink the outpoured wine.

The occasion becomes not only moving but also poignant before the brief service is concluded. Yesterday's Palestinian guerilla raid from Lebanon upon one of the Israeli border villages has provoked reprisal. As we take the bread and wine in obedience to the command and invitation of him who is Lord of Life and Prince of Peace, we hear the sound of Israeli planes flying over us on a revenge mission, and soon we hear the crump of their bombs, exploding in Lebanon some forty miles away. The prayers we are making for the peace of the Holy Land have deeper poignancy and more intense relevance because of this.

Throughout all the proceedings and alongside the noises of war, the indescribable beauty of the bird-song continues unabated. It elevates to grandeur our not very musical singing of 'When I survey the wondrous cross' and helps us carry away something of the very sound of heaven from that place.

We do not travel far to our next stopping-place—just a little way back along the road we have come and a swing left onto the road to Capernaum. In little more than a moment we turn off this road and draw up beside an unpretentious building which is the Church of the Loaves and the Fishes (known also as Tabgha). The miracle of the feeding of the five thousand almost certainly took place on the other side of the lake; but nevertheless this church commemorates the event, erected over the uncovered remains of a Byzantine church that stood here in the fourth century.

This early church, described in A.D. 386 by a pilgrim from Spain called Aetheria, was laid in ruins by the Persians in A.D. 614. Its remains were discovered in 1932 and subsequently the site was roofed over in the simple fashion that exists today.

That fourth-century church must have been a splendid thing. Its mosaic floor has to be seen to be believed. It is quite astonishing that it should have resisted so well the potential destruction of centuries, buried as it was beneath debris and undergrowth; and that its colours should have survived so wonderfully.

Along either side of the church the mosaic patterns represent quite marvellously the flora and fauna of the country. The creator of the mosaics must have had a fine love for nature as well as undoubted skill in putting together his little pieces of various coloured stone. He must have had a keen sense of humour, too.

Beautiful peacocks in green and blue are accompanied by other birds, beasts and flowers, all life-like and strangely appealing. I particularly like the one which shows a bird drinking from the water cupped in a lotus flower and another which represents two birds with a centipede strung between their two beaks, apparently in contention for the meal it represents.

The most impressive, and certainly the most famous, of all the mosaics is the one which is under the altar. This depicts five small loaves—shaped like our dinner rolls—in a basket, with a fish on either side. Here, too, the colours are still bright. It is one of the many romantic things to be met in the Holy Land, that after fourteen centuries these mosaics should be so fresh as they are today.

Next, we disembark a very short distance further along the Capernaum road and walk down to the Church of the Mensa Christi (sometimes known as the Church of the Primacy), standing right on the water's edge. This small church takes its name from the large, fairly flat-topped stone—itself the Mensa Christi or 'Table of Christ'—round which it was built of black basalt in 1943. It was on this very spot, so tradition claims, that Jesus had that post-Easter meal with his seven fishermen disciples in the dawn of a Lake Galilee day (John 21:1-13).

The Mensa Christi rock thrusts right across the altar space of the church and beyond the wall into the sea. A door beside it—cut to admit Pope Paul directly from the sea when he visited the spot in 1964—enables us to step out to the rock outside. There we see the steps hewn from the rock many centuries ago for the convenience of those arriving by boat. The Pope used them to come ashore to the specially made doorway directly above.

It is still only a little after ten o'clock in the morning. The sea is as calm as a millpond. In the sunshine it is like molten glass and so clear that we can see plainly a school of fish here and another there. It seems so appropriate as to be almost inevitable that we should sing part of the hymn, 'Dear Lord and Father of Mankind', particularly these two verses:

'In simple trust like theirs who heard,
Beside the Syrian Sea,
The gracious calling of the Lord,
Let us, like them, without a word
Rise up and follow Thee.

O Sabbath rest by Galilee!
O calm of hills above,
Where Jesus knelt to share with Thee
The silence of eternity,
Interpreted by love!'

Two miles further on is Capernaum, almost at the northern-most part of the lake. We mentioned that we meet many romances in the Holy Land. We encounter many ironies, too, and Caper-naum is one. In Jesus's time this was far and away the busiest town on the whole seaboard of Galilee. A very busy port and fishing town in its own right, it was also a centre of travel through which many routes had to pass. That is why it was the place where the tax-gatherer Matthew operated and, no doubt, many others of the same trade.

In Jesus's day Capernaum was always bustling with life and humming with activity. Today it is desolate and almost deserted. Nothing is here except some excavated ruins, a kiosk, a small Franciscan monastery and a jetty.

For Christian pilgrims, however, the very air of Capernaum breathes interest and excitement. Jesus spent much of his time here during his ministry in Galilee and this is the place that features so often in the stories about him that are recorded in the gospels. Foundations have been excavated which are claimed to have been the house of St. Peter—the very house in which Jesus sometimes resided.

There may be severe doubts as to whether this claim has as yet been sufficiently substantiated. There is however, little doubt as to the history of the other excavated ruins on the site. On the landward side of 'St. Peter's House' we see the partial reconstruction of an ancient synagogue.

It was just prior to the beginning of this century that Franciscans acquired this site, made some excavations and restored the synagogue to the limited extent that is before our eyes. It is generally accepted that this synagogue, while probably not the one that Jesus knew (built by the centurion of Luke 6:7), was the direct successor of that earlier building and erected on the same spot perhaps a century later, making use of many of the stones of the previous construction.

The pillars and carvings to be seen in the synagogue and the carvings on the many other excavated stones in the compound betray unmistakably Roman influence. Some of these carvings are specially noteworthy. We pay particular attention to one exquisitely carved representation of a conch shell enclosed within a laurel wreath and to another stone on which is carved a shield of David. Among other stones that we find interesting is one which bears the carving of a wagon which may be a picture of the Ark of the Covenant.

We notice, also, a large millstone among the relics in the compound. It makes us realise how terrible was Jesus's condemnation of any man who did despite to a child. Better for him, he said, to have a millstone tied to his neck and be cast into the depths of the sea (Matthew 18:6). When we see how massive this millstone is and think how quickly it must make a man plummet to the bottom of the sea, the warning strikes home in a way it never did before.

Instead of returning to the bus, we move to the jetty. We are going to take to the sea and sail to the kibbutz of Ein Gev on the west shore almost directly opposite Tiberias. We have arranged with the Kinneret Boat Company, based at Tiberias and linked with the kibbutz, to pick us up at Capernaum, ferry us to Ein Gev and later in the day return us to Tiberias.

Every Christian pilgrim to the Holy Land has his own favourite scenes and experiences. One of mine is to sail on the Lake. Since our Lord's day many things in the Holy Land have changed. This is inevitable, but sometimes the pilgrim cannot help regretting that this place or that has not been left just as it was when Jesus knew it. When he comes to the Sea of Galilee he finds his desire fulfilled.

Whatever other things have changed since Jesus's time on earth, here much is the same. The sea and its enclosing hills are just as he knew them. To sail on the waters that he sailed on so often and to look from the boat across the sea to the land in the certain knowledge that we are seeing much the same scene that he so often saw—that for me at least is an experience so precious that words could never match it.

Once our launch has moved out some distance from the jetty, we look back on the scene. We can see nothing of the synagogue; the trees that front it hide it from view. But on the hill to our left we can pick out the black dome of the Church of the Beatitudes. On our right we see the fissure in the hills where the River Jordan feeds itself into the sea. Further to our right, on the north-west of the lake, is the district of Gerasa, looking rather desolate still as it must have looked in that far off time when Jesus brought sanity to a violent madman just there (Mark 5:1-20).

We have the launch to ourselves on this trip and the captain readily agrees to stop the engines for a few minutes. As the boat drifts ever so gently in the calm sea, I read aloud the story of Jesus stilling the storm (Mark 4:35-41). In the short prayer that follows the presence of the living Christ is very real.

Some forty minutes sailing brings us to Ein Gev. Founded in 1937, Ein Gev is a kibbutz, that is, a collective settlement, of about four hundred members. From scratch the community that is Ein Gev has created a very pleasant, even lush, area out of desolation. Our guided tour and explanatory talk are fascinating. It is a delight to stroll among the palm trees and to see the variety of birds that flit around them, including the Turkish nightingale (or bulbul).

We conclude our conducted tour in the magnificent concert hall which has seating for two thousand and regularly houses concerts featuring international artistes. Its acoustics are first-class and before we leave it we once more join together in the singing of the twenty-third psalm to the tune Crimond.

When we emerge from the cool shade of our concert hall into the blazing heat of the early afternoon, there is just time for those of us so inclined to have a refreshing swim in the roped-off bathing area before we sit down together for lunch. The settlement has a restaurant on the lakeside, part of it indoors, part of it in the open-air. We are accommodated today in the open-air section, situated right over the water.

Everything served to us for lunch is the produce of the settlement. The main course is St. Peter's fish, caught in the lake, a delicacy that is with justification highly esteemed around the Sea of Galilee. This fish is more properly named the 'mousht' or 'comb' fish (*mousht* being Arabic for *comb*), the name coming from the shape of the large dorsal fin which resembles a comb. The more popular name, St. Peter's fish, derives from the tradition that it was in such a fish's mouth that Peter found the coin at the bidding of Jesus (Matthew 17:27).

Our homeward sail to Tiberias is scarcely less exhilarating than our trip from Capernaum was. We embark at three o'clock in the afternoon and find that the flat calm of the morning has given way to a mildly choppy surface.

On my first visit I observed exactly the same phenomenon on the day we visited Ein Gev. When I commented on this to one of the local inhabitants, he replied, 'Oh, yes, it happens like this every day in the summer. Always at three o'clock in the afternoon a breeze gets up'.

I was convinced my leg was being pulled but sure enough year after year I have found the phenomenon repeated. One theory is that it is all a matter of the heating up of the land with the advancing day. As the air is heated by contact with the hot land, it moves upwards and produces a breeze.

In any event, as we have sailed today on Lake Galilee, whether in a flat calm or through a little choppiness, we have been very conscious of the fact that Jesus was often abroad on this busy stretch of water; and without any exception we are aware that he is still abroad here.

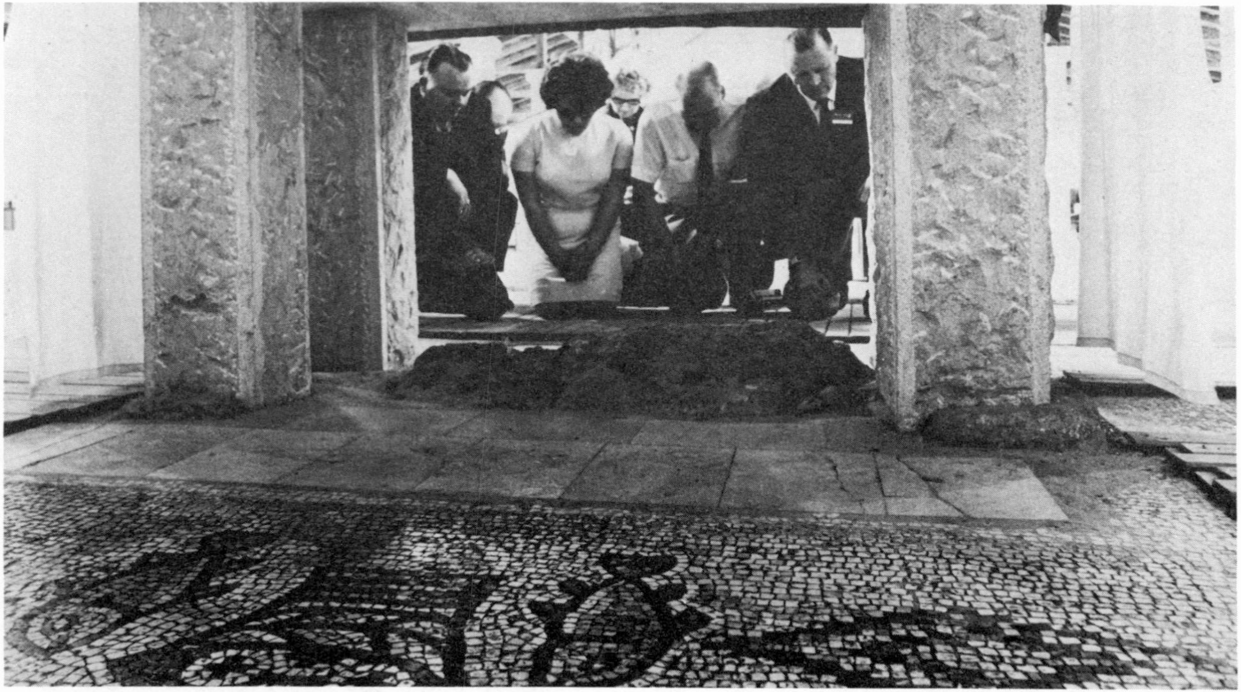

Plate 19. Loaves and Fishes Mosaic, Capernaum (*page 77*) *Courtesy Israel Government Tourist Office*

Plate 20. Synagogue at Capernaum (*page* 79)

Plate 21. Site of Paul's Prison. Caesarea (*page* 84)

CHAPTER TWELVE

Through Galilee to the Sea

Today we head for the Mediterranean, to visit Caesarea, Haifa and Acre. Apart from seeing these places, the trip will give us the opportunity of seeing something more of the topography of Galilee.

Galilee, of course, features much in the gospel narratives. Jesus spent nearly all of his earthly life in this province which was a very important district of the Middle East in his day. Its situation meant that it was in a real sense the crossroads of the world; the great routes all passed through Galilee. It was also by far the most fertile part of the country; its fertility, in fact, was proverbial. It was said that it was 'easier to raise a legion of olives in Galilee than to bring up a child in Judaea'.

Already, in our visit to Megiddo, centre of so many military conflicts, we have seen something of the consequences through the centuries of Galilee's strategic geographical situation. On today's journey to the coast through part of this quite small region—in all only some fifty miles long by twenty-five miles wide—we see something more of its lushness.

Following the road south along the lakeside we pass, about 1 $^1/_2$ miles from the Hospice, the Hot Springs, famous from ancient times for their healing properties. Soon we reach the south end of the lake and there, practically on the water's edge, is Degania, the first kibbutz to be founded in the country. That was in 1911.

It is very close to Degania that the River Jordan exits from the Sea of Galilee to flow on south until it empties itself eventually into the Dead Sea. The main road at this point runs for some yards almost on the verge of the river and bathing is not only permissible but reasonably feasible, provided one is happy enough to use the back of the bus as a dressing room. A number are eager to swim in the Jordan, or even across it, some want to fill bottles with Jordan water to take home and the rest are happy just to drink in the scene.

All in all, we have an enjoyable short stop here before continuing our journey. Leaving one sea behind us, we make our way towards another. Of our three ports of call on the Mediterranean, Caesarea is the first.

The excavated ruins of Caesarea are another of the many archaeological romances to be encountered in the Holy Land today. Twenty years ago practically nothing of what we now find before our eyes was showing above the sand.

Caesarea was a very important city of Palestine in Jesus's time and figures frequently in the narratives of Acts. Here lived that Cornelius whom Peter visited in response to his call for help (Acts 10); here lived Philip the evangelist to whose home came Paul with his companions en route to Jerusalem from Asia Minor; and, of course, it was here that Paul spent two years in prison after being taken into custody in Jerusalem and before sailing to Rome to face trial.

Founded by Herod the Great in 22 B.C. and named in honour of Augustus Caesar, Caesarea was the Roman capital in Palestine for about five hundred years. It then fell into near disuse and ruin until the Crusaders restored it in the twelfth century. The town they built was a great deal smaller than the previous Roman town but they erected a rampart which is still standing today, even though Caesarea was destroyed by the Moslems when they finally got rid of the Crusaders in A.D. 1291.

Thanks to the excavations of recent years, we are able to see a remarkable amount of Roman and Crusader Caesarea. Apart from the rampart already mentioned, there are parts of streets and archways and buildings of one kind and another. Just outside the town and quite near the main road is a ruin where stand two huge statues, both headless, discovered accidentally in 1954. Along the road to the north of the town are the massive aqueducts made by the Romans in the second century A.D. to carry sweet water from the mountain springs into Caesarea. By far their greater part is still beneath the sand but even that part exposed to view is fully a hundred yards in length; as it towers above us, close to the seashore and running parallel to it, it is very impressive.

Easily the most significant part of the Caesarea excavations for Christians is not even there for us to see. That may sound distinctly odd, so let me explain. To the south of Caesarea a Roman amphitheatre was excavated in 1961. This has now been largely restored and is regularly used for concerts. The acoustics, we discover, are remarkably good. When I stand on the stage and speak in a normal tone, I am heard quite distinctly by those of the party who are in the topmost stone seats in the auditorium.

The most significant thing to be upturned in those 1961 excavations was a stone bearing an inscription which mentions Pontius Pilate and the Emperor Tiberius. This archaeological evidence of Pilate's procuratorship is of profound importance. The actual stone is now in the museum at Jerusalem but at the entrance to the amphitheatre we see a facsimile.

At Caesarea we have our picnic lunch and some delightful swimming before we continue on our way. Amid the excavated ruins of the town is a cafe where we find it extremely pleasant to sit in the open air and eat our lunch while looking across the swimming beach and harbour to the new jetty, built, so it is believed, on the very spot where once stood the prison that housed the apostle Paul as he awaited ship to take him to Rome.

After lunch we board the bus and move on. Heading back to the main road, past enormous sand dunes and, surprisingly, a golf course—the very first in Israel, a sign tells us—we turn north towards Haifa.

Haifa is built on the slopes of Mount Carmel, the mountain where the prophet Elijah had his dramatically successful showdown with the prophets of Baal (1 Kings 18:17-38). To come in on Haifa from the sea, as I did once, to see the city clambering up the mountainside and the mountaintop high above smiling benevolently over it, is to catch a vision of holy grandeur that is a long time fading.

While the peak of the mountain rises above Haifa, and that is, of course, Mount Carmel proper, the mountain is regarded as extending far to the south. We are still many miles from Haifa when what nearly everyone in Israel refers to as 'The Carmel' begins to rise gradually higher and higher on our right hand side. With the mountain ascending steadily on one side and the sea never far from the road on the other, the drive towards Haifa is most pleasant.

One or two members of our group knew Haifa during the Second World War; when we reach the city they find it greatly changed since then. Now considerably enlarged, and Israel's chief seaport, it is the country's third largest city. Its population is around a quarter of a million; nearly all are Jewish but there are several thousand Christians and Moslems, as well as a number of Ba'hais.

Modern Haifa displays a distinguishable three-tier social structure in its housing—lowest, middle and highest, depending on how high up the mountain one's house is. The difference from one level to the next is plain to see as we drive steadily upwards from the level of the docks.

High on the mountainside, in the middle of the uppermost area, our bus stops at Panorama Point. Spread before us is one of the most magnificent sights imaginable. Haifa Bay must surely be one of the loveliest in the world, stretching in its semi-circle from the foot of Mount Carmel towards Acre, barely visible in the hazy distance.

Below us the scene is dominated by the striking golden dome of the Ba'hai Shrine. Founded in the middle of the nineteenth century in Persia, the Ba'hai religion is an admixture of bits and pieces taken from Mohammedanism, Christianity, Judaism and Zoroastrianism. Persecuted by the Persian government the Ba'hais eventually selected Haifa as their holy city—bringing the bones of their leader here for burial in 1909—and what we see below us is their central shrine.

Back in the bus, we begin the fifteen miles journey to Acre, hurrying past Haifa's diamond factory as soon as we are informed that no free samples are handed out to tourists. Leaving the centre of the city behind, we pass through Haifa's main industrial district. As we do so, we cross the River Kishon where Deborah defeated the Canaanites in battle and where today stand oil refineries.

We are now journeying through the valley of Zevulun and shortly we cross a bridge over the Naaman River. This was known as the River Belus to the Greeks and the Roman historian Pliny tells us that it was here, where the river reaches the sea, that a remarkable happening took place. A ship carrying a cargo of natron was wrecked at this point. The sailors lit a fire and used the natron rocks to support their cooking vessel over it. The heat melted the natron and the molten natron fused with the sand of the shore to produce glass. It was in this completely accidental fashion that glass was discovered.

Acre is little more than a mile further along the road. Known also as Akko (or Acco), it is nowadays in two parts, the Old Town and the New Town. It is, of course, the Old Town that commands our interest. One of the ancient cities of the world, Acre's importance goes back centuries before Christ. The city was known to the Greeks and Romans as Ptolemais and it is mentioned by that name in Acts 21 :7.

Around the year A.D. 1100 the Crusaders made what was then called Acco into the Christian stronghold and seaport which they named St. John of Acre because the Knights of St. John had their headquarters there. Acre was an important place then without a doubt; one eyewitness account of 1172 speaks of its harbour having no less than eighty ships lying at anchor. After the Crusaders were driven out of Jerusalem, Acre became the capital of the much reduced Christian Kingdom in Palestine. With this heavily fortified town as their centrepiece and bulwark the Christians dominated this coastal section of the Holy Land until the Moslem capture of Acre in A.D. 1291 finally put paid to the Crusader presence if not its influence.

In succeeding centuries the importance of Acre sometimes waxed and sometimes waned. The present century, particularly since the First World War and even more since the Second, has seen it having to yield more and more of its stature and importance to its neighbour, Haifa. The old town of Acre is today not much more than a relic of past glories.

At the same time it is an interesting and formidably impressive relic. When the Crusaders built anything they apparently intended it to last, if not for ever certainly for a very long time. As we walk round, we notice how well the massive fortifications, thrusting themselves bravely at the sea, have survived the passage of many hundreds of years, looking in most cases just as strong as the day they were completed.

One of the most fascinating things we see in Acre is St. John's Crypt. Only recently discovered and excavated, it is a remarkably well-preserved building erected by the Crusaders in the thirteenth century.

Pleasantly refreshed with lemon tea and cream cake at a cafe built over the water at the end of the Crusader sea wall we make back to Tiberias via Safed. Safed (or Sefad or Tsefat) is the highest inhabited spot in Israel. Thirty-three miles east of Acre and twenty-two miles north of Tiberias, it is built on Mount Canaan and the highest part of the town is more than three thousand feet above sea level.

The Crusaders, who seem to have been practically everywhere in the Holy Land, were here, too, and built fortifications on its heights in the twelfth century. On a clear day the vista presented from the heights of Safed is outstanding, with Lake Galilee to be seen on the south-east and Lake Hula on the north-east, backed by snow-capped Mount Hermon and linked to Lake Galilee by the River Jordan. By the time we reach Safed, however, the afternoon is so far advanced that the light is not good enough for us to see this picture. And so we proceed south, descending rapidly and passing the villages of Rosh-Pinna and Migdal before we skirt the Mount of Beatitudes and join the coast road which took us—was it only yesterday?—to those wonderful places at the north end of the lake and which now leads us back to the Scots Hospice.

CHAPTER THIRTEEN

Nazareth and Mount Tabor

When I announce at our evening meeting that tomorrow we will visit Nazareth, there is at once a murmur of excited—perhaps even awed—anticipation. This reaction does not surprise me. Nazareth, after all, was where Jesus spent by far the most of his earthly life.

Nazareth was proverbially an undistinguished backwater or even worse in Jesus's day. The New Testament narrative makes that clear. When Nathanael is told by Philip about this Jesus he has met who comes from Nazareth, his scorn for Nazareth is undisguised, 'Nazareth' he exclaimed, 'Can anything good come from Nazareth' (John 1 :45-46).

Of little intrinsic significance and even an object of some scorn as it was, Nazareth nevertheless occupied a remarkably interesting situation geographically. The hills which cradled the village overlooked the great Plain of Esdraelon. Then as now this was easily the most fertile area in the whole country. It was also a great thoroughfare along which passed traders of all countries and soldiers of many nations.

Nazareth in a very real sense stood at one of the world's great crossroads; and, even if she played little or no part herself in the affairs of men and nations going on around her, these things must have often occupied the mind of the boy Jesus growing to manhood in that place. Today the world still follows the ancient way of the sea that leads towards Nazareth; but now, instead of simply passing on to other more important places, it stops to look and often to pray.

Until very recently Nazareth was a completely Arab town, most of the population being Christian, the rest Moslem. Now there is a steadily growing Jewish community. The older part of the town, in the lower reaches, is still almost entirely Arab while the new housing in the upper reaches is inhabited by Jews.

We leave for Nazareth, only twenty miles distant from Tiberias, at our regular departure time of 8 a.m. Four miles short of our destination we come to the Arab village of Kefar-Kana which is usually identified with the Cana of Galilee where Jesus transformed water into wine (John 2:1-11). The village contains two Christian churches, a Greek Orthodox close to the highway and a Franciscan nearer the middle of the village. The Franciscan church is reputed to be built upon the site of the house where the miracle took place.

In order both to see this church and also to have a stroll through a typical Arab village, we get off the bus where a narrow street leads off the main road into the village. It is both pleasant and absorbing to walk leisurely through Cana of Galilee in the morning sun, and very soon we arrive at the church.

There is not a great deal to see inside the present church which is built over the site of an ancient one, some remains of which are visible in the crypt. Also to be seen is an old jar said to be just like those which featured in the miracle which Jesus performed on this very spot or its near vicinity.

When we leave the church, we do not retrace our steps but continue to follow the street along which we have been walking. In due course it brings us back to the main road, on the opposite side of the village to our point of entry—and there is the bus waiting for us, the driver enjoying some Turkish coffee at a little roadside cafe.

It is only a short drive from here to Nazareth. We pass over the brow of the hill with its mass of new houses that constitute the Jewish section of modern Nazareth and make our way down into the centre of the town. The main focus of our interest here is the breathtakingly beautiful Church of the Annunciation. Completed in 1966 this superb building stands over the traditional site of the announcement made to Mary that she was to bear a very special boy child (Luke 1:26-32).

The outside of the church is extremely lovely, its light-coloured stonework stretching heavenwards with such an appearance of eager freshness as must uplift many a heart. The loveliness inside even surpasses that of the exterior.

We first go in to see the lower church. This includes the traditional Grotto of the Annunciation and parts of the Crusader and Byzantine churches, which were two of those which previously stood on this same site. As a place of worship, the lower church is used mainly for special and for private masses.

The upper church, built directly over the lower and reached by a stairway embellished by some exquisite stained glass, is the parish church. We cannot help catching our breath in awe at its beauty and its worshipfulness. We are particularly struck by the wonderful mosaics, set in panels round the walls and the gift of various countries; and, perhaps most of all, by the dome which is in the shape of an opened lily inverted (Nazareth means 'lily'). Beneath that dome we have our short devotions, including the story of the Annunciation.

This is not by any means all there is to see in Nazareth or even all that we manage to see.

We visit the Church of St. Joseph, close to the Church of the Annunciation and erected over the traditional site of Joseph's shop and house.

We visit the Synagogue, belonging to the Greek Catholics. It is no longer a place of worship but a synagogue stood here in the sixth century, and it is very likely, therefore, to have been where the synagogue stood in Jesus's day. A large, bare room is all that remains of that sixth-century synagogue.

We visit the Church of the Adolescent Jesus standing on the hill-top high above the town and containing a striking figure of the boy Jesus above the high altar.

We walk through the Souk and feel again, as we did in ·Jerusalem, that this must even today be little different from what it was in Jesus's time.

Some of us pay a visit to the Edinburgh Medical Missionary Society Hospital high up on the hillside where we see something of that fine work in Christ's name among the Arabs which the Society has been doing in Nazareth for more than a hundred years. Then we sing a hymn in their splendid new chapel whose communion table is a working model of a carpenter's bench, operative side facing the congregation.

We have lunch in a Nazareth Restaurant on the main street and this, as on every tour, proves to be a highlight that takes the group by surprise. Despite its rather unprepossessing frontage the tables are spotless, the food is excellent and the enthusiastic *bonhomie* of our host is delightful.

After lunch and a brief skirmish with some of the shops, we are given the opportunity of a trip to the top of Mount Tabor and a visit to the church there. Most are anxious to accept although a few have their eyes fixed on some brasswork or other objects and opt to continue shopping.

Those of us for Tabor pile into the taxis which have been arranged and off we go. Mount Tabor is the traditional site of the Transfiguration (Matthew 17:1-8), although in this case the tradition goes no further back than the fourth century. Most authorities are convinced that it is much more likely that the Transfiguration actually took place on the slopes of Mount Hermon. They arrive at this conclusion for a number of reasons. Tabor is not a very high mountain (1,843 feet above sea level), neither was it the deserted place that the gospel narrative might seem to suggest. There is quite clear evidence that in Jesus's day Tabor was inhabited at least by a small garrison. Moreover, the Transfiguration appears to have occurred when Jesus and his disciples were in the far north of Galilee. It was soon after Peter's momentous confession at Caesarea Philippi—and Caesarea Philippi lay close to the foot of Hermon.

All in all, Mount Hermon seems to fit in much better than Mount Tabor as the site of the Transfiguration. Nevertheless, from the fourth century onwards countless pilgrims have regarded Tabor as commemorating that event and have climbed to its summit in recollection of it.

This afternoon we follow in their train—although with the expenditure of much less physical effort than the bulk of our predecessors. In previous centuries, and even into the present century, the regular, sometimes the only, means of ascending the steep mountainside was on foot. One of our group, with little head for heights, almost wishes she *was* afoot as the taxis whirl us past the village of Daburiya at the foot of Tabor and then round the succession of hairpin bends on the motor road that spirals up to the top.

It is an exhilarating journey. As we weave our way higher and higher the view of the plain spread out below becomes more and more enchanting.

Our taxis bring us to the very gates of the Franciscan church of the Transfiguration, built on the summit of the mountain. There are in fact two churches on Mount Tabor. Close beside the Franciscan church, but a little lower down the slope, is a Greek Orthodox church built in 1911. The Franciscan basilica is, however, much the more interesting.

The present church was built in 1921-23 on the self-same site previously occupied by Byzantine and Crusader churches. It enshrines remains of these earlier churches and contains some fine modern mosaics, particularly a representation of the Transfiguration. This is another of the numerous Holy Land churches of recent date whose acoustics make things difficult for the speaker but enhance group singing. And so, at the conclusion of our brief devotions—reading, of course, the Transfiguration story—we sing a hymn. The echoes rolling majestically round the church continue to reverberate in our minds long after we have descended the mountain.

Before we leave, however, we survey the scene from the mountain-top. When we come outside, we go round the side of the church and up some steps onto the roof of an old building. This brings us to the very brink of the precipice and presents us with a wonderful view of the Plain of Esdraelon far below with, to the north, the mountains of Galilee and just a glimpse of snow-peaked Hermon and, to the south, the mountains of Samaria.

The descent is at least as exhilarating as was the ascent and the drive back to Nazareth allows us to recover our breath before joining up with the 'remnant' for the return to Tiberias. For much of the journey Tabor, with the Franciscan Church perched on top, is clearly in our view. The mountain is in fact the dominating feature of the topography of the area. So toweringly dominating is it indeed that it is quite startling to reflect that

Mount Tabor is considerably lower on the earth's surface than Jerusalem, which is 2,500 feet above sea level. This is an interesting thought with which to end the day's touring.

CHAPTER FOURTEEN

Caesarea Philippi and the Golan Heights

The next two days are free and are spent quite blissfully—strolling leisurely here and there, completing the shopping, basking in the sun, lying in the shade, swimming in the sea, sipping cool drinks at lakeside cafes. The day following, which is Sunday and our last day before departure home, we accept the offer of an optional trip to Caesarea Philippi and to the Golan Heights.

Since it is Sunday and also the last full day we are ever likely to spend together, we begin it with a Communion service on the lawn of the Hospice. Even at seven o'clock in the morning it is already warm and we are glad of the shelter offered by the many trees in the garden. Once more the birds sing for us and with us as we celebrate the Sacrament beside that sea which our Lord knew so well.

After breakfast we take again, and for the last time, the road to the north end of the lake—past the Mount of Beatitudes, past Tabgha and on this occasion past Capernaum as well. We are on a new road now, new since the 1967 War. Shortly we come to a bridge and we ride across the Jordan near to the spot where it flows into Lake Galilee.

Now we travel north and east through the battle areas, scenes of conflict in the 1967 and 1973 wars. 'It was just here' says our Israeli driver, for instance, and his words are all the more dramatic because they are uttered in a matter-of-fact tone, 'It was just here that we turned the Syrian advance in 1973. This was the furthest point they reached'.

By this time we are well and truly on the Golan Heights. Signs of past battles and of present military occupation are plentiful. Mount Hermon comes into view and almost immediately Kuneitra is in sight.

Kuneitra is presently in no-man's-land and we cannot go right into the town. We are near enough, however, to see how truly it is described as a ghost town. Its windows peer sightlessly back at us out of empty houses, for all the world like eyesockets in a dead skull. This is what was, before the Six Days' War, the most important town in the region and the headquarters of the Syrian Army. Now it is deserted.

Close beside Kuneitra is the buffer zone manned by the United Nations peace-keeping force, made up of detachments from six countries, three on the Israeli side and three on the Syrian. By now Hermon looms very large and very close, its majestic appearance enhanced by the snow on its peaks and in its gulleys. With this holy mountain as its backcloth, the scene before us of the two United Nations' manned frontier posts and the fifty yards stretch of road between is one of great poignancy.

We proceed a few miles further, pass by a Druze village with the interesting name of Masada, and turn off the main road for a mile or two to Birket-Ram, a delightful natural pool in the crater of an extinct volcano. (The name Birket-Ram means Height Pool). Here we are almost on the lower slopes of Mount Hermon. From this point indeed skiers make their way up the mountain to enjoy its winter snow. From Birket-Ram the view of Mount Hermon, now closer, is even more imposing. No wonder it has commanded so much admiration and reverence down the centuries; this highest of all the Holy Land's mountains, 9,232 feet above sea level, stands partly in Syria, partly in Lebanon and partly in Israel.

We are now only seven miles from Banyas, the Caesarea Philippi of the New Testament. After the ever-welcome refreshment interlude at the fine café overlooking the crater pool, we move on there. On the way we notice a fortress standing incongruously but proudly on a high prominence to our right. It is a stronghold that the Crusaders built in the 12th century as protection against the Moslems in Damascus, and is known as Nimrod.

At Banyas rises one of the two chief sources of the River Jordan—there are other two lesser sources: the River Dan and the River Senir in Hatsbani. Perhaps because the great river found its origin here, perhaps because of the sheer natural loveliness of the spot, Banyas has been a place of veneration and worship from earliest known times.

It is reckoned to have been one of the main centres of Baal worship in primitive days and perhaps to have been the 'Baal-Gad under Mount Hermon' of Joshua 11:17, 12:7, 13:5. The Greeks in their turn made it a place of worship and dedicated a shrine there to Pan, calling the place Paneas after the god.

Herod the Great—he seems to have been as ubiquitous as the Crusaders and as indefatigable in building—was given this district by the Emperor Augustus in 20 B.C. and erected a white marble temple to his honour close to the shrine of Pan. His son, Philip, tetrarch of the region, followed this up by enlarging the town and naming it Caesarea in honour of the Emperor Tiberius, adding Philippi (Philip's Caesarea) to distinguish it from that other Caesarea on the Mediterranean coast.

Agrippa II changed the official name of the place to Neronias but the earlier titles of Paneas and Caesarea continued in use and they survived when Neronias died out. In time Caesarea also fell out of use, leaving Paneas in possession of the field, a possession which it has effectively retained to the present day. The modern designation of Banyas is simply an Arabic corruption of the old name, due to the fact that the Arabs have no '*p*' in their language.

When the road suddenly bursts through the trees and our eyes light upon the spot where Caesarea Philippi once stood, we understand at once how from time immemorial men have felt this place casting a spell over them. It is exceedingly lovely.

Out of the high reddish-coloured cliff in front of us gushes a fast flowing stream of water, already large enough to justify its title of river, River Banias. The dedication to Pan by the Greeks of this grotto where the Jordan source takes its rise is evidenced by the inscriptions to be seen in niches both inside it and close by on the cliff face.

Our return to Tiberias is by a different, and shorter, route. Turning westwards as we leave Banyas, we pass Tel Dan, the site of the ancient city which was the furthest north habitation in Biblical Palestine. The familiar saying 'from Dan to Beersheba' indicated the whole length of the country because Dan was the northernmost, as Beersheba was the southernmost, city of the land.

Six miles further brings us to Kiryat-Shemona, a very young town, close to the Lebanese border. It was given its name, which literally means 'Town of the Eight', in memory of eight young people who lost their lives in the defence of nearby Tel-Hai during the War that followed the cessation of the British Mandate and the creation of the State of Israel in 1947.

Turning south at Kiryat-Shemona and aiming for Tiberias, we traverse the side of the Hula Valley. There are three main bodies of water in the Jordan rift, that great geological fault in the earth's surface which cleaves the Holy Land from top to bottom. Two of them we have already come to know fairly well—the Dead Sea and the Sea of Galilee. Lake Hula is the third—and the smallest.

The River Jordan flows into Lake Hula in the north and leaves it in the south to flow on to the Sea of Galilee. Until the State of Israel came into being, the Hula Valley was almost entirely unproductive marsh land. Years of hard work have resulted in the swamps being drained and today the Hula Valley is extremely fertile. Here it has come literally true that the desert has blossomed like the rose (Isaiah 35:1).

Passing by the site—and excavations—of biblical Hazor, we reach Rosh-Pinna which was a frontier post between Palestine and Syria in the days of the British Mandate. At this point we join once more the road that takes us past Migdal and the Mount of Beatitudes to the Sea of Galilee and our temporary home in the Church of Scotland Hospice.

Today's tour has, advisedly, been neither long nor strenuous because tomorrow promises an early departure and preparations have to be made. There is time, therefore, this Sunday afternoon, to do whatever last day things each wants to do—some walk, some shop, some sit, some swim, all reflect and, sooner or later, all pack.

At the usual after-dinner meeting for devotions and administration, we are conscious of the fact that it is extremely unlikely that this group of people from many parts, and many nations even, will ever again be gathered together in one spot on the earth. But we are glad and grateful for the real fellowship we have enjoyed in our pilgrimage together; and our hope is firmly confident that someday we will all meet again in heaven.

All the group members, of whatever denomination, proceed this Sunday evening to the weekly service of worship in the simple little building, very near to the water's edge, that is the Church of Scotland. Service over, a number spend a last contemplative half-hour at the lakeside café, imprinting indelibly on their memories the sounds of the water lapping gently against the sea wall beneath their feet and of the fish plop-plopping softly back into the lake after they rise to feed; and the sight of the fishing boats riding at anchor just off the shore, with the lights of Ein Gev twinkling on the opposite bank.

EPILOGUE: ALL OVER?

Everyone is up and about early enough to see the sun coming up on the Sea of Galilee—an unforgettable sight. The early rise is necessary because breakfast is at 4.30 and the bus departs for Ben Gurion Airport at 5.15. This enables us to drive at a comfortable speed and still arrive the two hours before take off that security regulations demand. It also allows us to enjoy our last look at Galilee in the freshness of the early morning and, as we skirt Tel Aviv and draw near to the airport, to witness Israel hurrying to its day's work.

The security checks, tedious though they are even when their necessity is recognised, are conducted with efficiency and courtesy. Although it is now approaching departure time, those of us who have flown several times before know that the aircraft will not leave exactly on schedule and that, therefore, there is ample time to spend our remaining Israeli coins on tea and cake at the buffet counter (our paper money already having been changed at the airport bank into dollars or sterling, since we are not supposed to take Israeli currency out of the country).

We are on the point of attacking our much needed snack when a rather unwelcome voice summons our flight to the boarding gate—and a whole row of steaming cups of tea and cream cakes is sadly abandoned. In a few minutes we are aboard. Shortly we are airborne and our last view of the Holy Land is the glimpse we catch through the aircraft windows as we fly over Tel Aviv and the coastline to strike across the Mediterranean for home.

As we settle back in our seats, many of my fellow pilgrims are saying to themselves, 'Well, that's it'. There is still the journey home to enjoy. There are still entrancing views to be caught of the Mediterranean, dazzlingly blue in the sun, of Crete, of the Greek Islands, of the Italian coast, of the Alps, of Mont Blanc, of the French countryside, of the English Channel—and many things besides. But, they muse sadly, the pilgrimage is over.

During these two weeks, the experience was so marvellous that it often seemed as if it could never come to an end. Now it has and the realisation plucks at their heartstrings.

For my part I am hoping that they will soon recall what I said to them, as leader, at our final group meeting last night. Our time together in the Holy Land has come to a close as we all knew it must. But the pilgrimage we have shared will never end. The Bible, our faith, life itself, have all been given a new dimension which we can never lose.